GOURMET LOW GI

hamlyn

GOURMET LOW GI

Azmina Govindji

First published in Great Britain in 2006 by Hamlyn,
a division of Octopus Publishing Group Ltd
2–4 Heron Quays, London E14 4JP

Copyright © Octopus Publishing Group Ltd 2006

Distributed in the United States and Canada by Sterling
Publishing Co., Inc., 387 Park Avenue South, New York,
NY 10016-8810

ISBN-13: 978-0-600-61504-0
ISBN-10: 0-600-61504-9

A CIP catalog record for this book is available from the
British Library

Printed and bound in China

10 9 8 7 6 5 4 3 2 1

Notes
Nutritional analyses are given per serving. Where a recipe
has split servings (e.g. "serves 6–8,") the analysis is given for
the first figure.

The FDA advises that eggs should not be consumed raw. It
is prudent for more vulnerable people such as pregnant and
nursing mothers, invalids, the elderly, babies, and young
children to avoid uncooked or lightly cooked dishes made
with eggs.

Meat and poultry should be cooked thoroughly. To test if
poultry is cooked, pierce the flesh through the thickest part
with a skewer or fork—the juices should run clear, never
pink or red.

This book includes dishes made with nuts and nut
derivatives. It is advisable for those with known allergic
reactions to nuts and nut derivatives and those who may be
potentially vulnerable to these allergies, such as pregnant
and nursing mothers, invalids, the elderly, babies, and
children, to avoid dishes made with nuts and nut oils. It is
also prudent to check the labels of preprepared ingredients
for the possible inclusion of nut derivatives.

Standard level spoon measurements are used in all recipes.

Fresh herbs should be used unless otherwise stated.

Where pepper is listed in the recipe ingredients, always use
freshly ground black pepper.

Medium eggs should be used unless otherwise stated.

Ovens should be preheated to the specified temperature—
if using a convection oven, follow the manufacturer's
instructions for adjusting the time and the temperature.

The information in this book should not be considered
as a replacement for professional medical advice. A
physician should be consulted in all matters relating to
health and especially in relation to any symptoms that
may require diagnosis or medical attention.

CONTENTS

INTRODUCTION

You've probably picked up this book because you've heard a little about GI—glycemic index—and want to embrace the health benefits a low-GI diet can offer, even when you're entertaining and indulging yourself a little. You may be interested in GI because you or someone close to you has developed diabetes and you are aware of the beneficial effects GI has on blood-sugar or glucose levels. Or, possibly, you have just flicked through the pages that follow and noticed the enticing recipes and helpful nutritional notes. Whatever the reason for your interest, choosing low-GI foods can promote a healthy lifestyle, for you, your friends, and your family.

Before we think about why the idea of GI is valuable when you are watching your health or your waistline, we need to know what GI actually means.

The glycemic index is all about what happens to your food once it's left your fork. When you eat a carbohydrate (such as bread, potatoes, pasta, cereals, and sugary foods) your body digests it and converts it into glucose (sugar), which can be used for energy. As the carbohydrate gets converted into glucose, the glucose level in your blood rises. GI is simply a ranking of carbohydrate foods based on the speed at which they raise blood-glucose or sugar levels after they have been digested. Each food is given a value:

- Carbs that break down quickly are given high values. They raise blood glucose quickly and have a high GI.
- Carbs that break down slowly are given low values. They raise blood glucose slowly and have a low GI.

Low-GI carbs, such as whole grains, beans, lentils, pasta, nuts, seeds, fruit, and vegetables, are inherently healthy, and experts agree that these foods can make a valuable contribution to your diet. You don't need to know the GI ratings or values of individual foods in order to eat the low-GI way. Simply choose to have a low-GI food at each meal or snack, swapping your usual foods for the lower-GI versions as often as you can (see the lists on page 10 for some ideas).

The recipes that follow will give you plenty of ideas for meals using low-GI ingredients. They are designed to be easy to make and include store-bought ingredients, such as olives in herb-flavored brine and ready-crushed ginger. These will save you time but give delicious results. To save you even more time we have also included some menu suggestions (see page 11) that will help you combine the dishes within the book for various occasions, including a Summer lunch al fresco for six, a Sunday lunch for four, and a Winter warmer for six.

THE FUSS ABOUT GI

When your blood glucose rises your body releases a hormone—insulin—from the pancreas. Insulin reduces your blood-glucose levels by directing glucose from the blood either to your muscles (where it can be used for energy) or to fat stores (where it is stored as fuel for another time). The more quickly a food raises blood-glucose levels, the higher its GI rating and the greater the insulin response. Research has suggested that if your blood-glucose levels are constantly high, your blood-insulin levels are consequently high, and this can lead to a condition known as insulin resistance (IR). IR can make you more prone to metabolic syndrome (Syndrome X), type-2 diabetes, and coronary heart disease, especially if you are overweight. This is one of the key reasons why low-GI foods and meals can help you keep in good overall health.

Imagine eating a slice of multigrain bread. You have to chew the grains first, which takes more time than if you were to chew white or even whole-wheat bread. The multigrain bread is also digested more slowly than white and whole-wheat breads. This affects the speed at which they raise blood glucose. As a result, the GI rating of seeded breads, such as multigrain, are lower than—and preferable to—white and even whole-wheat bread. Whole-wheat is, of course, a better source of fiber than white bread, but in terms of GI it acts in pretty much the same way as white.

Blood-glucose levels respond differently to high- and low-GI foods. With a high-GI food the rapid rise in blood glucose is followed by a quick fall, which is associated with hunger. So, low-GI foods may actually help prevent hunger pangs, which is great news if you are watching your weight.

HOW TO GI YOUR DINNER TABLE

Identifying the GI of foods requires specific laboratory analysis, and not all foods have been analyzed, even if they do contain carbs. If we were to assess the GI values of the recipes in this book, we would get an accurate measure only if we were to feed a group of people a measured amount of each dish. We would then, under laboratory conditions, test their blood-glucose response over a period of time and compare this to the same amount of carbohydrate found in pure glucose—an expensive, laborious, and unnecessary process! To keep it simple, these recipes have been carefully designed to include a selection of tasty yet low- to medium-GI ingredients. The way a dish is cooked, how long it's cooked for, what it is served with, whether you squeeze some lemon juice on top, and more, will affect the GI of the food. This knowledge has been carefully integrated into the recipes.

You will see that many of the recipes are dressed in lemon or lime juice or have a scattering of sesame seeds or a handful of nuts, all of which help to lower the GI of the finished dish.

In order that these recipes are super-tasty yet nutritious, you'll notice that they use reduced-fat ingredients, such as plain, strained yogurt instead of cream, lean meats, and monounsaturated oils, such as olive and canola, which are better for you.

So, go on, treat yourself—and your friends—to one of my scrumptious, nutritious, low-GI gourmet meals any day of the week!

Low-GI foods

Eat the following foods often—they are your best friends:

- **Grainy breads,** such as multigrain, soy and linseed, and softgrain white

- **Porridge and granola**

- **Pasta**—any type—cooked until *al dente* and smothered in tomato-based sauce (even a basic one from a jar)

- **Vegetables galore**—raw ones are the best, but if you cook them, keep them firm

- **Fruits,** especially apples, pears (even canned ones in natural juice), strawberries, and peaches

- **Basmati rice, sweet potato, couscous, and new potatoes cooked in their skins**

- **Beans**—choose from kidney beans, chickpeas, baked beans, and lentils; even canned chili beans get a GI gold star

- **Lean meat, fish, and poultry;** eat egg, Quorn™, tofu, and nuts if you prefer vegetarian main meals

- **Nuts** (yes nuts!)—eat a handful a day to help manage your weight and lower your blood-cholesterol levels

GI swaps for breakfast

Instead of this ... →	... have this
• Cornflakes, rice-based cereals, sugar-rich cereals	• Branflakes, cereals with dried fruit, oat-based cereals, such as porridge and granola
• White or whole-wheat bread	• Multigrain or other seeded bread
• Fruit juice	• Fresh fruit, such as grapefruit
• Jam	• Peanut butter

GI swaps for lunch

Instead of this ... →	... have this
• Baguette or bagel, whole-wheat or white bread	• Whole-grain bread, wheat tortilla wrap, rye bread, pitta bread, multigrain bread
• Hummus	• Chickpea salad
• Potato salad	• Pasta salad
• Pureed soup	• Soup with whole beans or lentils

GI swaps for dinner

Instead of this ... →	... have this
• Roast or mashed potato	• Boiled new potatoes in their skins
• Jasmine or risotto rice	• Basmati, brown, or long-grain rice
• Sweet or oily dressing	• Acidic dressing based on lime or lemon juice
• Baked potato	• Baked yam, cassava, or sweet potato

GI swaps for snacks

Instead of this ... →	... have this
• Chocolate bar	• A handful of nuts
• Rich dessert	• Fruit, yogurt, dried fruit, regular ice cream
• Digestive cookies, soda crackers, or rice cakes	• Oat-based crackers, oat-based cookies
• Cake	• Fruit loaf or currant bun

MENU SUGGESTIONS

Meal for two

Grilled Haloumi with Sun-dried Tomatoes (see page 22)

Seared Tuna with Lemon Salsa (see page 47)

Garlic, Roasted Bell Pepper, and Walnut Pappardelle (see page 84)

Sizzling Bananas with Orange Zest and Pistachio Nuts (see page 138)

Summer lunch al fresco for six

Salmon Mousse on Pumpernickel (see page 16)

Rosemary Lamb Shanks with Red Onions and Spiced Beans (see page 55)

Caramelized Green Beans (see page 114)

Chinese Spiced Citrus Salad (see page 130)

After-work supper with friends for six

Buttered Asparagus Spears with Toasted Sesame Seeds (see page 27)

Fillet of Sole with Butter and Dill (see page 38)

Fragrant Cinnamon Basmati Rice (see page 112)

Sautéed Okra with Onion Seeds and Saffron (see page 119)

Bitter Chocolate Almond Mousse (see page 128)

Winter warmer for six

Cauliflower Cheese Soup with Toasted Pumpkin Seeds (see page 14)

Braised Oxtail with Orange (see page 74)

Almond and Apricot Wild Rice with Cumin Seeds (see page 91)

Ginger Broccoli with Fennel Seeds (see page 109)

Baked Pear with Almond Crisp (see page 124)

Sunday lunch for four

Stuffed Garlic Mushrooms with Feta Cheese (see page 25)

Plaice en Papillotte with Fennel and Chili (see page 51)

Fruity Couscous with Lime (see page 116)

Cherry Granola with Macadamia Nuts (see page 126)

Family supper for four

Beef Tikka with Tamarind Dipping Sauce (see page 24)

Japanese-style Salmon Steaks (see page 46)

Stir-fried Noodles with Portobello Mushrooms (see page 101)

Baked Saffron Peaches with Mango and Cream (see page 136)

Amazing Appetizers

CAULIFLOWER CHEESE SOUP
with toasted pumpkin seeds

Preparation time: 15–20 minutes

Cooking time: 1¼ hours

Serves 6

2 tablespoons vegetable oil

1 onion, finely chopped

1 large cauliflower, about 2½ lb, cut into florets

½ cup sharp Cheddar cheese, grated

black pepper

VEGETABLE STOCK

1 lb mixed vegetables (excluding potatoes, parsnips, and other starchy root vegetables), chopped

1 garlic clove, thinly sliced

6 peppercorns

1 bouquet garni

5 cups water

TO SERVE

2 tablespoons pumpkin seeds

4 tablespoons low-fat plain, strained yogurt

CARBOHYDRATE 9 g

FAT 10 g

PROTEIN 12 g

ENERGY 167 kcal/695 kJ

1 Make the vegetable stock. Put all the ingredients in a large saucepan. Bring to a boil and simmer gently for 30 minutes, skimming if necessary. Strain the stock through a muslin-lined sieve, return to the saucepan, and keep warm. These ingredients will make a little more than 4 cups, and any stock not used in this recipe can be chilled then frozen for use in other dishes.

2 Meanwhile, heat the oil in a large saucepan and fry the onion. Cook gently until soft but not browned. Add the cauliflower florets, cover, and cook for 5–10 minutes. Stir in 4 cups of the vegetable stock and simmer for 30 minutes until the cauliflower is tender.

3 Lightly toast the pumpkin seeds in a dry, nonstick skillet. They will start to pop when they are ready, but keep watch while they toast because they can easily burn.

4 Puree the soup in a food processor or rub through a sieve and return it to the saucepan. Add the cheese and season with black pepper. Reheat thoroughly until the cheese melts through the soup. If wished, add more liquid, such as hot stock or vegetable water to thin the soup.

5 Serve in warm bowls with a swirl of yogurt and a sprinkle of toasted pumpkin seeds.

Nutrition notes

The pumpkin seeds add a crunchy texture as well as being a good source of minerals and healthy omega-3 fats.

Choosing a sharp cheese means you can use less and also reduces the need for extra salt.

SALMON MOUSSE
on pumpernickel

Preparation time: 25 minutes, plus setting

Serves 8

14½ oz poached salmon, any bones removed

¼ cup low-fat crème fraîche

⅔ cup low-fat ricotta cheese

1 tablespoon chopped dill, plus extra dill leaves for garnish

4 tablespoons lemon juice

1 egg white

½ oz leaf gelatin (about 4 sheets)

1 teaspoon vegetable oil

black pepper

mixed salad greens, to garnish

TO SERVE

4 slices dark pumpernickel bread, quartered

4 lemons, cut into wedges

CARBOHYDRATE 8 g

FAT 12 g

PROTEIN 16 g

ENERGY 206 kcal/860 kJ

1 In a large bowl, flake the salmon and then beat in the crème fraîche, ricotta, dill, lemon juice, and black pepper. Mix well.

2 Whisk the egg white until peaks form. Melt the gelatin in 3–4 tablespoons very hot, but not boiling, water. Stir the gelatin into the fish mixture and then carefully fold in the egg white.

3 Coat the insides of 8 molds or ramekin dishes with a little oil to prevent the mousse from sticking. Spoon the fish mixture into the molds or ramekin dishes, cover with plastic wrap and place in the refrigerator for 2–3 hours to set.

4 Remove the mousse from the molds or ramekin dishes by sliding a knife around the edges to loosen, then turn them upside down.

5 Garnish with the extra dill leaves and some mixed salad greens and serve with quarters of pumpernickel bread and lemon wedges.

Poaching salmon Use a large piece of salmon, such as the tail end. Put the salmon in a large pan or fish kettle, add a bay leaf, parsley sprigs, a bouquet garni, 10 whole black peppercorns, and water to cover. Bring to simmering point and cook for 2 minutes. Turn off the heat and leave, covered, to cool. The residual heat in the water will poach the salmon. Do not remove the lid until it is completely cool (at least 5 hours). Lift the salmon from the poaching liquor and remove any skin and bones.

Nutrition notes

Pumpernickel bread has a lower GI than other breads, and its flavor marries well with oily fish.

Fresh salmon is a wonderful source of omega-3 fatty acids, which help lower blood triglycerides, a risk factor in heart disease.

PANEER CUBES
with cumin and baby spinach

Preparation time: 5 minutes

Cooking time: 3–4 minutes

Serves 4

1 tablespoon canola oil

2 teaspoons cumin seeds

7 oz Indian paneer cheese, cut into ½-inch cubes

¼ teaspoon ground turmeric

¼ teaspoon paprika

2 cups baby spinach leaves

juice of 1 lime

salt and black pepper

CARBOHYDRATE 1 g

FAT 19 g

PROTEIN 5 g

ENERGY 191 kcal/800 kJ

1 Heat the oil in a nonstick wok or skillet and add the cumin seeds. Allow them to pop over a low heat for a few seconds.

2 Stir in the cheese, turmeric, and paprika, season to taste, and cook for 3–4 minutes until lightly browned.

3 Toss the cheese mixture with the spinach leaves and lime juice and serve immediately.

Nutrition note

Although it is sometimes called cottage cheese in Indian restaurants, paneer is actually a high-fat cheese, so don't go overboard on this one!

HONEYED FIGS
with raspberries and goat cheese

Preparation time: 3 minutes

Cooking time: 3 minutes

Serves 4–8

8 fresh figs, preferably black

1 tablespoon honey

¾ cup raspberries

3 oz reduced-fat goat cheese, cut into 4 thin slices

a handful of flat-leaf parsley, chopped, to garnish

CARBOHYDRATE 17 g

FAT 3 g

PROTEIN 4 g

ENERGY 108 kcal/460 kJ

1 Halve the figs, put them on a foil-lined broiler rack and drizzle the center of each one with a drop of honey. Cook under a preheated hot broiler for 2–3 minutes.

2 Garnish with the flat-leaf parsley and serve hot on individual plates alongside the goat cheese and the raspberries.

Nutrition note
This tempting appetizer contributes one serving toward the daily fruit and vegetable intake recommended by the U.S. Department of Health and Human Services and Department of Agriculture's (USDA) Dietary Guidelines for Americans.

HOT CHICKEN LIVER SALAD

Preparation time: 5 minutes, plus soaking
Cooking time: 5 minutes
Serves 4

13 oz chicken livers, trimmed and halved
⅓ cup milk
2 teaspoons thyme leaves
1 tablespoon olive oil
2 garlic cloves, crushed
1 red chili pepper, sliced thinly (optional)
7-oz can water chestnuts, drained and halved

TO SERVE
7 oz Belgian endive, leaves separated
1½–2 tablespoons balsamic vinegar

CARBOHYDRATE 9 g
FAT 10 g
PROTEIN 21 g
ENERGY 199 kcal/835 kJ

1 Soak the liver in milk for 30 minutes to remove any bitterness. Discard the milk and pat the liver dry with paper towels. Sprinkle the chopped thyme over both sides of the liver.

2 Heat the oil in a large skillet and add the garlic and sliced chili, if using. Allow the garlic and chili to soften for 30 seconds and then add the chicken livers and water chestnuts.

3 Cook over a medium heat for 3–4 minutes, until the liver is browned on the outside but still pink in the middle.

4 Serve on bed of crispy raw Belgian endive, drizzled with balsamic vinegar and with any remaining pan juices.

Nutrition note
Chicken livers are an excellent source of iron, protein, and B vitamins.

GRILLED HALOUMI
with sun-dried tomatoes

Preparation time: 5 minutes

Cooking time: 10 minutes

Serves 4

7 oz haloumi cheese, sliced

2 teaspoons onion seeds

1 tablespoon finely chopped cilantro leaves

a few saffron threads

arugula leaves, to garnish

TO SERVE

¾ oz sun-dried tomatoes in oil, drained and sliced

½ orange, peeled and pith removed, separated into segments

2 tablespoons lemon juice

CARBOHYDRATE 3 g

FAT 15 g

PROTEIN 11 g

ENERGY 186 kcal/778 kJ

1 Place the cheese slices on a foil-lined broiler rack and sprinkle over the onion seeds, cilantro leaves, and saffron.

2 Preheat the broiler and cook the cheese under a moderate heat for 4–5 minutes on each side until it is soft and slightly browned.

3 Serve immediately on a bed of sliced sun-dried tomatoes and orange segments. Drizzle the lemon juice over the cheese just before serving, and garnish with a few arugula leaves.

Nutrition notes

Tomatoes are a rich source of the antioxidant lycopene, known for its anticancer properties.

Haloumi cheese is naturally high in salt, so there is no need to add any extra in this recipe.

BEEF TIKKA
with tamarind dipping sauce

Preparation time: 10 minutes, plus marinating

Cooking time: 5 minutes

Serves 4

⅔ cup low-fat plain yogurt

1½ tablespoons tandoori spice mix

10-oz beefsteak, cut into 1-inch cubes

2 teaspoons vegetable oil

½ teaspoon onion seeds

1 teaspoon crushed ginger

2 tablespoons chopped cilantro leaves

DIPPING SAUCE

1 teaspoon tamarind paste

3 tablespoons warm water

1 tablespoon chopped cilantro leaves

2 teaspoons finely chopped chives

½ teaspoon red chili powder

salt and black pepper

CARBOHYDRATE 5 g

FAT 6 g

PROTEIN 18 g

ENERGY 140 kcal/590 kJ

1 Mix together the yogurt and tandoori spice mix and marinate the beef in the mixture for 30 minutes.

2 Meanwhile, make the dipping sauce by mixing together all the ingredients. Season to taste.

3 Heat the oil in a skillet and add the onion seeds. Allow them to pop over a low heat for a few seconds. Stir in the ginger and add the marinated beef together with any juices.

4 Cook for about 5 minutes until the meat is just tender. Stir in the cilantro leaves. Serve immediately accompanied by the dipping sauce.

Nutrition note
Yogurt and tandoori mixes can be used as a low-fat way of spicing up fish and chicken dishes, too.

STUFFED GARLIC MUSHROOMS
with feta cheese

Preparation time: 10–12 minutes

Cooking time: 20 minutes

Serves 4

4 large portobello mushrooms

2 teaspoons olive oil

1 small onion, finely chopped

2 garlic cloves, crushed

2½ oz feta cheese, finely diced

1 tablespoon chopped cilantro leaves and stems

1 tablespoon chopped basil leaves

8 pitted olives, halved

black pepper

mixed salad greens, to serve

CARBOHYDRATE 2 g

FAT 5 g

PROTEIN 3 g

ENERGY 67 kcal/276 kJ

1 Peel and remove the stalks from the mushrooms. Finely chop the stalks and sauté them in hot oil in a skillet with the onion and garlic for 3–4 minutes until soft.

2 Mix the feta with the mushroom and onion mixture, add the herbs, and season with some black pepper.

3 Arrange the mushroom caps, flat-side down, on a greased baking pan and spoon the onion mixture on the top.

4 Lay the olives on top of this and cook in a preheated 350°F oven for 20 minutes until browned. Serve immediately on a bed of mixed salad greens.

Nutrition note

Feta cheese is naturally salty, so there is no need to add extra salt to this recipe.

BUTTERED ASPARAGUS SPEARS
with toasted sesame seeds

Preparation time: 3–5 minutes
Cooking time: about 15 minutes
Serves 6

1 lb asparagus spears
1 tablespoon olive oil
2 tablespoons butter
4 teaspoons sesame seeds
1 teaspoon wholegrain mustard

CARBOHYDRATE 2 g
FAT 8 g
PROTEIN 3 g
ENERGY 90 kcal/372 kJ

1 Snap off any woody asparagus stems by bending the end of the spears. Heat the oil and butter in a flat, heavy skillet.

2 Place asparagus spears in the skillet in a single layer to cover the base of the skillet and cook for about 5 minutes, until just tender and slightly charred. You may have to cook the asparagus in several batches.

3 Meanwhile, heat a nonstick skillet and toast the sesame seeds for a few seconds, turning them with a wooden spoon until they start to brown.

4 Stir the mustard into the asparagus and serve immediately, topped with the toasted sesame seeds.

Nutrition note
One serving will give you almost three-quarters of your daily requirement of folic acid, a B vitamin. Folic acid, or folate, helps reduce risks of heart disease, stroke, and cancer.

AVOCADO AND SMOKED SALMON
with sunflower seed salad

Preparation time: 10 minutes

Serves 2

2 slices smoked salmon, about 3½ oz each

1 small, firm avocado, sliced into wedges

juice of ½ lime

2 teaspoons low-calorie mayonnaise

1 teaspoon wholegrain mustard

2 tablespoons chopped dill

TO SERVE

1¼ cups arugula leaves

2 teaspoons sunflower seeds

CARBOHYDRATE 3 g

FAT 20 g

PROTEIN 29 g

ENERGY 305 kcal/1270 kJ

1 Wrap the smoked salmon slices around the sliced avocado and sprinkle with lime juice.

2 Mix the mayonnaise with the mustard and dill.

3 Serve the wrapped avocado on a bed of arugula with the mustard mayonnaise. Sprinkle with sunflower seeds.

Nutrition note

Avocado, although rich in fat, contains the more beneficial type of monounsaturated fat.

THAI CHICKEN SALAD
with basil and peanut dressing

Preparation time: 10 minutes

Cooking time: 15–20 minutes

Serves 4

5 oz cooked chicken breast, shredded

3 tablespoons cilantro leaves

2 cups (5 oz) bok choy, shredded

DRESSING

1 tablespoon peanut oil

1 tablespoon Thai fish sauce

juice of 1 lime

juice of 1 small orange

1 garlic clove, crushed

3 tablespoons roughly chopped basil leaves

¼ cup unsalted peanuts, skins removed and chopped

black pepper

TO GARNISH

2 scallions, green stems only, shredded lengthwise

1 plump red chili, seeded and sliced diagonally

CARBOHYDRATE 4 g

FAT 7 g

PROTEIN 16 g

ENERGY 144 kcal/604 kJ

1 Make the dressing by shaking all the ingredients together in a screw-top jar.

2 Mix the chicken with the cilantro leaves and stir in the dressing.

3 Line a serving dish with the bok choy, spoon the dressed chicken on top, and serve chilled, garnished with scallion shreds and red chili slices.

Nutrition notes

Chicken breast is one of the lowest-fat meats.

Peanuts add valuable monounsaturated fat, vitamin E, and a range of important minerals to this recipe. A handful of peanuts as part of a balanced diet can help lower blood-cholesterol levels and help you manage your weight.

GRILLED EGGPLANT
with chili toasts

Preparation time: 15 minutes

Cooking time: 10 minutes

Serves 4

2 eggplant, about 1 lb 2 oz in total

2 teaspoons olive oil

2 oz sun-dried tomatoes in oil

2 garlic cloves, crushed

4 tablespoons lemon juice

CHILI TOASTS

4 slices multigrain bread

1 tablespoon chili-infused oil

TO GARNISH

4 basil leaves

black pepper

CARBOHYDRATE 15 g

FAT 6 g

PROTEIN 4 g

ENERGY 122 kcal/513 kJ

1 First, prepare the chili toasts. Remove the crusts from each slice of bread and cut the remaining bread into two neat triangles. Brush each side of the bread with the chili-infused oil and put the bread on a baking pan.

2 Cut each eggplant lengthwise into slices ¼ inch thick and season with black pepper.

3 Put the chili toasts in a preheated 425°F oven and cook for 8–10 minutes until crisp and golden.

4 Meanwhile, oil a grill pan and heat it. Put the eggplant slices and sun-dried tomatoes on the grill pan with the garlic and cook for about 4 minutes until they start to soften. Turn over the eggplant and cook for a further 4 minutes. Add the lemon juice.

5 Remove the chili toasts from the oven. Serve with the eggplant and tomato piled high in the center of each plate, garnished with basil leaves, and sprinkled with black pepper.

Nutrition notes

These Mediterranean vegetables are full of great antioxidants, which will help your body's immune system.

Multigrain breads have a lower GI than either whole-wheat or white bread.

Fantastic
Fish

SCALLOPS IN PANCETTA
on lemon lentils

Preparation time: 15 minutes
Cooking time: 45 minutes
Serves 4

16 scallops, about 13 oz in total, roe removed
2 tablespoons chopped oregano leaves
7 oz pancetta, cut into 16 thin slices

LEMON LENTILS
1 teaspoon olive oil
1 onion, chopped
6 cloves
1⅙ cups Puy lentils, washed
1⅔ cups Vegetable Stock (see page 14)
1⅓ cups hot water
⅛ teaspoon asafetida
4–6 tablespoons lemon juice
black pepper

TO GARNISH
mixed salad greens
1 lemon, cut into 4 wedges
⅔ cup low-fat plain, strained yogurt sprinkled with lemon zest
handful of oregano leaves

CARBOHYDRATE 36 g
FAT 16 g
PROTEIN 47 g
ENERGY 467 kcal/1967 kJ

1 Prepare the lemon lentils by heating the olive oil in a saucepan over medium to low heat. Add the onion and cook for about 5 minutes, stirring occasionally, until it begins to brown. Add the whole cloves and lentils and cook for 5 minutes.

2 Pour in the vegetable stock, measurement water, and the asafetida and bring to a boil. Simmer gently, uncovered, for 30 minutes until the lentils are tender.

3 Meanwhile, sprinkle the scallops with the chopped oregano and wrap each in a slice of pancetta. Thread 4 scallop parcels onto a skewer. Repeat with the remaining scallops. Grill the scallops on a barbecue or under a preheated hot broiler for 2–3 minutes each side until they are golden brown.

4 Remove and discard the cloves from the lentils and stir in the lemon juice and black pepper. Serve garnished with mixed salad greens, a lemon wedge, and yogurt, and sprinkled with oregano leaves.

Nutrition note
Lentils are packed with soluble fiber and are valuable for keeping blood-sugar levels evenly balanced. They also help to keep the GI content of the meal down as well as providing a tasty, filling alternative to rice.

FILLET OF SOLE
with butter and dill

Preparation time: 10 minutes

Cooking time: 10–15 minutes

Serves 4

4 sweet potatoes, about 1½ lb in total, sliced

1 tablespoon olive oil

2 tablespoons all-purpose flour

3¼ cups dill, chopped

4 sole fillets, about 1¼ lb in total

¼ cup butter

4 tablespoons lemon juice

salt and black pepper

CARBOHYDRATE 49 g

FAT 16 g

PROTEIN 29 g

ENERGY 443 kcal/1868 kJ

1 Boil the sweet potatoes in lightly salted water for about 5 minutes until just tender. Drain, drizzle with the olive oil, and keep warm.

2 Mix together the flour and dill with some seasoning. Coat each fillet with this seasoned flour.

3 Heat the butter in a large skillet and pan-fry the fish for about 3 minutes on each side.

4 Serve the fish, drizzled with lemon juice, on the still warm sliced sweet potatoes.

Nutrition note
Sweet potatoes are a good source of the antioxidant vitamin betacarotene, and they have a lower GI rating than standard potatoes.

BAKED TROUT FILLET
with toasted pine nuts

Preparation time: 5 minutes

Cooking time: 15–20 minutes

Serves 4

1 trout fillet, about 1¼ lb

1½ cups dill, roughly chopped

3 scallions, sliced

1–2 teaspoons lemon pepper

1 tablespoon pine nuts

salt

mixed salad greens, to serve

1 orange, peeled, pith removed, and sliced, to garnish

CARBOHYDRATE 4 g

FAT 10 g

PROTEIN 3 g

ENERGY 222 kcal/935 kJ

1 Place the trout fillet, skin-side down, on a foil-lined baking pan. Sprinkle the dill, scallions, lemon pepper, and salt over the trout fillet and cover tightly with foil.

2 Bake the trout in a preheated 400°F oven for 15–20 minutes.

3 Meanwhile, toast the pine nuts in a heavy skillet for 1–2 minutes.

4 Sprinkle the toasted pine nuts over the trout and serve on a bed of mixed salad greens, garnished with slices of orange.

Nutrition note

Trout is rich in natural omega-3 fatty acids, which are known to protect the heart. Because it is an oily fish, there is no need to add extra fat for cooking.

PAN-FRIED HALIBUT
with papaya and cilantro salsa

Preparation time: 20 minutes

Cooking time: 10–12 minutes

Serves 4

2 teaspoons olive oil

3 garlic cloves, crushed

4 halibut steaks, about 1¼ lb in total

salt and black pepper

watercress leaves, to serve

SALSA

1 papaya, cut into cubes

½ red onion, finely chopped

1 cup cilantro leaves, finely chopped

¼–½ teaspoon red chili powder

1 red bell pepper, cored, seeded, and finely chopped

juice of ½ lime

CARBOHYDRATE 20 g

FAT 6 g

PROTEIN 28 g

ENERGY 236 kcal/993 kJ

1 Heat the oil in a large, nonstick skillet. Add the garlic and stir for a few seconds. Put the fish steaks in the skillet and fry for 10–12 minutes until just cooked, turning halfway through cooking.

2 Meanwhile, make the salsa by mixing together all the ingredients.

3 Serve the halibut steaks on a bed of watercress, with the salsa on the side.

Nutrition notes

Using salmon instead of halibut in this recipe will boost your intake of omega-3 fat.

The chunky papaya and bell peppers, together with the acidic lime, help lower the glycemic index of any other carbohydrates that you may be serving to accompany this dish.

MONKFISH TERIYAKI

Preparation time: 15 minutes

Cooking time: 15–20 minutes

Serves 4

2 garlic cloves, crushed

¾-inch piece ginger root, peeled and shredded

2 dessertspoons reduced-salt soy sauce

½ teaspoon rice wine vinegar

1¼-lb monkfish tail, bones removed, and cubed

1 tablespoon chopped chives, to garnish

ROASTED ASPARAGUS

1⅔ cups asparagus tips

1 tablespoon olive oil

BEAN SPROUT SALAD

heaping 1½ cups bean sprouts

2½ oz hot pickled pimiento peppers, drained and finely sliced

CARBOHYDRATE 5 g

FAT 4 g

PROTEIN 28 g

ENERGY 162 kcal/682 kJ

1 Mix together the crushed garlic, ginger, soy sauce, and rice wine vinegar.

2 Put the monkfish cubes in a nonmetallic ovenproof dish and pour over the soy sauce mixture. Cover with a lid.

3 Arrange the asparagus tips in a shallow roasting pan and spoon over the olive oil. Shake to coat but do not cover.

4 Roast both the fish and the asparagus in a preheated 400°F oven for 15–20 minutes.

5 Meanwhile, mix the bean sprouts with the pimiento peppers.

6 Arrange the bean sprout salad in the center of the plates and top with the monkfish. Pour over the hot fishy juices and garnish with chopped chives. Serve with the roasted asparagus.

Nutrition notes

White fish contains little fat and should be roasted in liquid to keep it moist.

Using reduced-salt soy sauce imparts a wonderful flavor and helps avoid overdoing the salt, which has been linked with high blood pressure.

CARIBBEAN MACKEREL
with avocado salsa

Preparation time: 30 minutes, plus marinating

Cooking time: 5 minutes

Serves 4

4 mackerel fillets, about 1½ lb in total

juice of 6 limes

½ cup dark rum

1 lime, sliced, to garnish

AVOCADO SALSA

2 medium tomatoes, about 9 oz in total

1 medium avocado, finely chopped

½ small red onion, finely chopped

1 tablespoon chopped cilantro

juice of 1 lime

a few drops of Tabasco sauce

CARBOHYDRATE 5 g

FAT 39 g

PROTEIN 37 g

ENERGY 577 kcal/2394 kJ

1 Make 2–3 small slashes in the flesh of each mackerel fillet so that the marinade will penetrate. Place the fish in a shallow dish.

2 Mix together the rum and lime juice and pour it over the mackerel. Place the mackerel in the refrigerator for 2–3 hours, removing it and turning it in the marinade every 30 minutes.

3 Make the salsa. Skin the tomatoes by cutting a cross in the bottom of each one. Pour boiling water over them and leave for 1 minute before draining and slipping off the skins when they are cool enough to handle. Cut each tomato in half and, holding it cut-side down over a plate, squeeze gently to extract the seeds. Chop the tomato flesh as finely as possible.

4 Combine the tomatoes and avocado with the onion and cilantro in a bowl with the lime juice and Tabasco. Cover and leave for at least 1 hour for the flavors to mingle and develop.

5 Remove the mackerel from the marinade and cook under a preheated hot broiler for 5 minutes. Serve accompanied by the avocado salsa and garnished with sliced lime.

Nutrition note

Avocado and oily fish are both rich in fat, but the good news is that this is healthier, monounsaturated, fat. Both foods also contain a wealth of vitamins.

CHUNKY MUSSEL SOUP

Preparation time: 35 minutes

Cooking time: about 45 minutes

Serves 4

1 tablespoon olive oil

6 oz shallots, sliced

1 garlic clove, finely chopped

2 bay leaves

2 lb mussels in their shells, prepared (see note below)

1 tablespoon chopped tarragon

1 tablespoon chopped thyme

1 tablespoon chopped oregano

a good pinch of saffron

1 cup bean sprouts

scant 2 cups baby spinach leaves

1 cup less 2 tablespoons low-fat plain, strained yogurt

FISH STOCK

3 lb fish trimmings (from any fish except oily fish)

1 onion, sliced

1 small leek, white part only, sliced

1 celery stalk, chopped

1 bay leaf

6 parsley stalks

10 whole peppercorns

2 cups dry white wine

7½ cups water

TO SERVE

2 tablespoons chopped parsley

8 slices sourdough bread

CARBOHYDRATE 26 g

FAT 7 g

PROTEIN 20 g

ENERGY 239 kcal/1010 kJ

1 Make the fish stock. Put all the ingredients in a large saucepan. Bring slowly to just below boiling point and simmer gently for 20 minutes, removing any scum that rises to the surface. Strain the stock through a muslin-lined sieve, return to the pan, and keep warm. The ingredients above will make about 7½ cups, and any stock not used can be chilled then frozen for use in other dishes.

2 Meanwhile, heat the oil in a large, deep pan and add the shallots, garlic, and bay leaves. Cover and cook for 6 minutes to soften.

3 Put the mussels in the pan and add 4 cups of the hot fish stock. Bring to a boil, cover, and cook on a fairly high heat, shaking the pan occasionally, for 3 minutes until the mussels have opened. Discard any mussels that are still closed.

4 Use a slotted spoon to transfer half the mussels in their shells to large, shallow soup bowls. Keep warm. Remove the remainder of the mussels from their shells and add them to the soup bowls.

5 Add the herbs, saffron, bean sprouts, and spinach to the stock remaining in the pan. Boil for 3 minutes, reduce the heat, and stir in the yogurt.

6 Discard the bay leaves and ladle the stock over the mussels. Sprinkle with chopped parsley and serve with sourdough bread to soak up the liquid.

Preparing mussels Scrub the mussels under cold, running water and pull or scrape off any tufts of hair (known as the beard) that protrude from the shell. Tap any mussels that are slightly open with the back of a knife and discard them if they do not close. Also discard any mussels that float in liquid or have broken shells. Make sure that you discard any mussels that have not opened after cooking.

JAPANESE-STYLE SALMON STEAKS

Preparation time: 5 minutes, plus marinating

Cooking time: 10 minutes

Serves 4

4 salmon fillets, about 1½ lb in total

4 oz dried flat rice noodles

2 tablespoons sesame oil

4 star anise

4 scallions, green stems only, sliced thinly lengthwise, to garnish

MARINADE

scant ¼ cup Japanese soy sauce

½ teaspoon wasabi paste

4 tablespoons teriyaki sauce

4 tablespoons rice wine vinegar

1-inch piece ginger root, peeled and shredded

1 teaspoon black pepper

CARBOHYDRATE 27 g

FAT 28 g

PROTEIN 37 g

ENERGY 514 kcal/2140 kJ

1 Make the marinade. Mix together all the ingredients and use the mixture to coat the fish. Set aside for at least 20 minutes.

2 Cook the noodles in lightly salted boiling water for 2–3 minutes or according to package instructions.

3 Heat 1 tablespoon of the sesame oil in a heavy, nonstick skillet and fry the star anise for a few seconds to release the aroma.

4 Carefully place the salmon, skin-side down, in the pan, adding any remaining marinade juices. Fry gently on each side for 3–4 minutes.

5 Meanwhile, heat the remaining oil and stir in the noodles to heat them through.

6 Serve the salmon on a bed of noodles, garnished with crisscross strips of scallion.

Nutrition note

Salmon is an oil-rich fish, and you should aim to eat oily fish once a week.

SEARED TUNA
with lemon salsa

Preparation time: 30 minutes, plus marinating

Cooking time: 5 minutes

Serves 4

4 tuna steaks, about 13 oz in total, cut about ¾ inch thick

3 garlic cloves, finely chopped

1 teaspoon fennel seeds, finely ground using a mortar and pestle

2 small dried red chilies, crumbled

1 tablespoon olive oil

4 tablespoons lemon juice

LEMON SALSA

1 large beefsteak tomato, about 8 oz in total, skinned, seeds removed (see page 43), and finely chopped

1 small red onion, finely chopped

1 garlic clove, crushed

½ green chili, seeded and chopped

2 tablespoons lemon juice

grated zest from 1 unwaxed lemon

1⅔ cups cilantro leaves, chopped

a pinch of sugar

TO GARNISH

grated zest from 1 unwaxed lemon

a handful of watercress leaves

CARBOHYDRATE 5 g

FAT 8 g

PROTEIN 25 g

ENERGY 190 kcal/799 kJ

1 Place the tuna steaks on a cutting board and rub half the garlic into one side of the steaks, followed by half the ground fennel seeds and one of the chilies. Turn the steaks over and repeat the process on the other side with the remaining garlic, fennel, and chili.

2 Place the fish in a shallow container and pour over the olive oil and lemon juice. Cover and leave to marinate for 1 hour.

3 Meanwhile, make the lemon salsa. Combine all the ingredients together in a bowl and put to one side to let the flavors develop.

4 Preheat a grill pan or barbecue grill to very hot and sear the tuna for 1–2 minutes on each side. The tuna should be pink in the middle when it is served. If you prefer it cooked through, cook for an additional 2 minutes on each side.

5 Serve the tuna hot with the lemon salsa and garnished with watercress leaves and the lemon zest.

BUTTERFLY SHRIMP
with zucchini ribbons

Preparation time: 30 minutes, plus marinating

Cooking time: 5 minutes

Serves 4

3 7-inch long zucchini (about 14½ oz in total), topped and tailed and sliced into fine ribbons with a vegetable peeler

28 raw, shelled, large shrimp with tails still intact, heads removed

a handful of chopped flat-leaf parsley, to garnish

MARINADE

a large pinch of saffron threads

8 tablespoons lemon juice

6 garlic cloves, roughly chopped

2 tablespoons rice wine vinegar

4 tablespoons olive oil

2 tablespoons drained capers

CARBOHYDRATE 6 g

FAT 12 g

PROTEIN 12 g

ENERGY 175 kcal/728 kJ

1 Make the marinade. Mix together all the marinade ingredients, lightly crushing the capers against the side of the bowl.

2 Place the zucchini ribbons in a large bowl and spoon two-thirds of the marinade mixture on top. Marinate for 3–4 hours.

3 Prepare the shrimp. Hold the tail underside up and cut each shrimp in half lengthwise. Pull out any black intestinal thread, rinse, pat dry on paper towels, and put in a shallow dish. Alternatively, ask your fishdealer to prepare the shrimp for you. Pour the remaining marinade over the shrimp and marinate for 3–4 hours.

4 Place the zucchini in a large skillet with their marinade and simmer over a medium-low heat for 3–5 minutes.

5 Grill the shrimp for 3–4 minutes until pink and sizzling, basting with the marinade. Be careful not to overcook them.

6 To serve, pile the zucchini in the center of a warmed dish, top with the shrimp and garnish with chopped parsley.

Nutrition notes

These delicious zucchini are an elegant substitute for pasta and help lower the GI content of the meal.

Shrimp do contain cholesterol, but it is saturated fat that is more likely to raise your blood cholesterol rather than the cholesterol that is found in shrimp.

PLAICE EN PAPILLOTTE
with fennel and chili

Preparation time: 30 minutes

Cooking time: 10 minutes

Serves 4

1 fennel bulb, about 12 oz

2 red chilies, seeded and chopped

4 tablespoons lemon juice

2 teaspoons extra virgin olive oil

4 plaice fillets, about 1 lb 6 oz in total

1 small handful chopped dill

½ lemon, cut into wedges, to garnish

RADICCHIO AND ORANGE SALAD

4 cups red radicchio leaves

2 large oranges, peeled and pith removed, separated into segments

CARBOHYDRATE 13 g

FAT 6 g

PROTEIN 32 g

ENERGY 234 kcal/988 kJ

1 Finely chop the fennel bulb and put it in a bowl with the chopped chilies. Add the lemon juice and olive oil and set aside.

2 Cut 4 sheets of parchment paper, each one about 14 x 7 inches, and fold them in half widthwise. Lay one half of a sheet over a plate and arrange a fish fillet on one side of the fold. Sprinkle over some chopped dill and fold over the paper to enclose the filling. Fold in the edges and pleat to secure. Repeat with the remaining fish.

3 Place the wrapped fish on a baking pan and cook in a preheated 425°F oven for about 8 minutes or until the paper is puffed up and brown.

4 Make the salad. Combine the radicchio with the orange segments.

5 Place each fish parcel on a large plate and cut an X-shaped slit in the top, or pull the paper apart to open the parcel, releasing a fragrant puff of steam, and curl back the paper. Serve with individual side bowls of the fennel and chili mixture and radicchio and orange salad, and garnish with a lemon wedge.

Nutrition notes

Fresh fish is very low in fat.

Oranges are a good source of vitamin C, an important antioxidant vitamin.

Mouthwatering Meat

ROSEMARY LAMB SHANKS
with red onions and spiced beans

Preparation time: 10 minutes, plus marinating

Cooking time: 2–2½ hours

Serves 4

4 lamb shanks, about 2½ lb in total, fat removed

4–5 rosemary sprigs

2 garlic cloves, thinly sliced

4 small red onions, halved

3 tablespoons balsamic vinegar

MARINADE

small bunch of thyme, leaves removed from stalks

3 whole cardamom pods

1 bay leaf

a pinch of saffron threads

4 tablespoons lemon juice

salt and black pepper

SPICED BEANS

2 teaspoons canola oil

½ teaspoon black mustard seeds

½ teaspoon onion seeds

1 tablespoon tomato paste

pinch of ground turmeric

¼–½ teaspoon red chili powder

2 x 10-oz cans pinto beans, drained

2 tablespoons chopped cilantro leaves, plus extra to serve

CARBOHYDRATE 10 g

FAT 14 g

PROTEIN 33 g

ENERGY 293 kcal/1230 kJ

1 Place the lamb shanks in a large roasting pan, make slits in each shank, and insert sprigs of rosemary and slices of garlic inside.

2 Make the marinade. Mix all the ingredients together. Coat the lamb shanks with the marinade, cover with foil and put in the refrigerator for at least 1 hour.

3 Cook the lamb in a preheated 325°F oven for 2–2½ hours, basting every 45 minutes or so, until the meat is tender.

4 Meanwhile, prepare the beans. Heat the oil and cook the mustard and onion seeds over a low heat, allowing them to pop for a few seconds. Stir in the tomato paste, turmeric, and chili powder and mix well. Add the beans, stir well, and add a few tablespoons of hot water. Cover and allow to cook for a few minutes. Stir in the chopped cilantro leaves and remove from the heat.

5 Preheat the broiler. Place the halved onions, cut-sides up, in a heatproof dish, pour over the vinegar, and cook under a medium heat for about 20 minutes until they are soft.

6 Serve the lamb accompanied by the spiced beans and broiled red onions and sprinkled with chopped cilantro leaves.

Nutrition note

Lean lamb is a good source of zinc and also of iron, which is available in a form that is readily absorbed.

LAMB SHANKS
with roasted new potatoes

Preparation time: 20 minutes, plus resting

Cooking time: 3 hours

Serves 4

4 lamb shanks, about 10 oz each

6–8 tablespoons lemon juice

¼ teaspoon dried oregano

¼ teaspoon dried thyme

2 oregano sprigs

4 lemon thyme sprigs

salt and black pepper

ROASTED NEW POTATOES

1 lb small new potatoes, skins left on

2 teaspoons olive oil

2 oregano sprigs

4 lemon thyme sprigs

2 bay leaves

2 large beefsteak tomatoes, about 1 lb in total, thickly sliced

CARBOHYDRATE 24 g

FAT 14 g

PROTEIN 32 g

ENERGY 347 kcal/1460 kJ

1 Put 2 large sheets of foil crosswise in a roasting pan. These will make a large sealed envelope to steam the meat in its own juices.

2 Remove any skin and excess fat from the lamb shanks and place them in the lined roasting pan. Sprinkle the lemon juice, dried herbs, salt, and some black pepper evenly over the meat. Tear the leaves from the oregano and thyme sprigs and put them around the meat.

3 Fold over the foil to form a sealed parcel and cook in a preheated 350°F oven for 3 hours.

4 Put the new potatoes in a flat roasting dish and roll them in the olive oil to coat. Tear the leaves from the oregano and thyme sprigs and lay the slices of beefsteak tomatoes over the top. One hour from the end of the cooking time for the meat, put the potatoes and tomatoes, uncovered, in the oven.

5 When the meat is cooked remove it from the oven and leave it to rest for 10 minutes. Remove the bay leaves from the caramelized potatoes and tomatoes before serving alongside the lamb shanks, drizzled with any remaining cooking juices.

Nutrition note

New potatoes are lower in GI than many other types of potato, and leaving the skins on provides extra fiber.

EXOTIC LAMB BROCHETTES

Preparation time: 15 minutes, plus marinating

Cooking time: 5–10 minutes

Serves 4

1 lb lamb loin, cut into small cubes

juice of 2 kiwifruit

16 chestnut mushrooms

16 oyster mushrooms

1 teaspoon olive oil

4 garlic cloves, crushed

1 tablespoon finely chopped rosemary

TO SERVE

1 lemon, cut into wedges

8 pitta breads, warmed

mixed salad greens

CARBOHYDRATE 45 g

FAT 13 g

PROTEIN 34 g

ENERGY 423 kcal/1785 kJ

1 Put the lamb cubes in a shallow dish, pour the kiwifruit juice over the meat, and marinate for 2–3 hours.

2 Brush the mushrooms with the oil. Thread the marinated lamb cubes onto 8 skewers, alternating with the two different types of mushroom. Scatter the crushed garlic and chopped rosemary over the brochettes.

3 Cook under a preheated hot broiler or on a barbecue for 5–10 minutes, turning occasionally so that the brochettes cook evenly.

4 Serve with lemon wedges, warmed pitta breads and mixed salad greens.

Nutrition notes

Mushrooms, particularly Asian types, contain compounds that are reputed to stimulate the immune system and may help reduce blood-cholesterol levels.

Pitta bread has a more favorable GI than white bread or baguette.

LAMB NOISETTES
with herb crust on tangy lima beans

Preparation time: 10 minutes

Cooking time: 15–20 minutes

Serves 4

2 tablespoons finely chopped mint

1 tablespoon finely chopped thyme

1 tablespoon finely chopped oregano

½ tablespoon finely chopped rosemary

4 teaspoons wholegrain mustard

4 lamb noisettes, about 4 oz each

mixed salad greens, to serve (optional)

TANGY BUTTER BEANS

2 teaspoons vegetable oil

1 medium onion, chopped

1 tablespoon tomato paste

scant ¼ cup pineapple juice

2 tablespoons lemon juice

a few drops of Tabasco sauce

black pepper

1½ cups cooked lima beans or drained canned beans

CARBOHYDRATE 14 g

FAT 14 g

PROTEIN 32 g

ENERGY 305 kcal/1280 kJ

1 Mix together all the chopped herbs in a bowl. Spread mustard on both sides of each noisette and dip the meat into the herb mixture. Press the herbs firmly to the mustard. Chill the lamb in the refrigerator until you are ready to cook.

2 Make the tangy lima beans. Heat the oil in a skillet and fry the onion until it has softened. Add the rest of the ingredients to the skillet and cook gently for 5 minutes.

3 Preheat the broiler to hot and cook the lamb noisettes for about 4 minutes each side. The lamb should be cooked but still retain a slight pink colour.

4 Serve the lamb immediately surrounded by the tangy lima beans and accompanied by mixed salad greens, if liked.

Nutrition notes

The delicious lima beans that replace potato in this recipe keep the GI of the meal low.

Serve some lightly steamed green vegetables with the meal to lower the GI even further.

CHERMOULA CHICKEN

Preparation time: 45 minutes, plus marinating

Cooking time: 1 hour

Serves 4

2 lb chicken pieces on the bone (such as thighs, legs, or quarters), skin removed

chopped parsley, to garnish

SPICE MIX

1 large onion, finely chopped

2 large garlic cloves, finely chopped

½ teaspoon ground cumin

¼ teaspoon paprika

¼–½ teaspoon crushed dried chilies

1–2 pinches of saffron threads

6 tablespoons finely chopped cilantro

6 tablespoons finely chopped flat-leaf parsley

2 tablespoons olive oil

2 tablespoons lemon juice

PEARL BARLEY

1 teaspoon vegetable oil

1 small onion, chopped

1 cup pearl barley, washed

4 cups hot Chicken Stock (see page 69)

RAITA

⅔ cup low-fat plain yogurt

4-inch piece of cucumber, grated

pinch of ground cumin

CARBOHYDRATE 52 g

FAT 13 g

PROTEIN 30 g

ENERGY 428 kcal/1800 kJ

1 Combine all the ingredients for the spice mix in a bowl. Rub the spice mix all over the chicken flesh. Set the chicken aside for at least 2 hours to absorb the flavors.

2 Prepare the pearl barley. Heat the oil in a large, heavy skillet and cook the onion gently until soft, stirring so it does not brown. Add the washed barley and cook for 2 minutes. Pour in the hot stock and simmer for 1 hour, stirring occasionally, until all the fluid has been absorbed and the grains are soft.

3 Meanwhile, cook the chicken, uncovered, in a preheated 375°F oven for 30–40 minutes until it is tender throughout.

4 Make the raita. Combine the yogurt and grated cucumber and sprinkle some cumin on the top.

5 When the chicken and pearl barley are cooked, garnish the chicken with chopped parsley and serve immediately with the pearl barley and raita.

Nutrition notes

Removing the skin from the chicken not only reduces the fat content considerably but also has the advantage of allowing the spice flavors to penetrate the chicken flesh.

Pearl barley is often overlooked in cooking, yet it has a low GI of only 25 and is high in soluble fiber.

MOROCCAN LAMB AND PRUNE TAGINE

Preparation time: 35 minutes, plus marinating

Cooking time: 5¼–5¾ hours

Serves 4

2 cups Beef Stock (see page 74)

1½-lb leg of lamb, fat removed, cubed

1 tablespoon olive oil

1 large onion, finely chopped

2 medium tomatoes, chopped

¾ cup ready-to-eat prunes

scant ¼ cup whole almonds, roughly chopped

½ teaspoon saffron threads

½ cup flat-leaf parsley, chopped

scant 2 cups cilantro leaves, chopped

couscous, to serve (optional)

MARINADE

½ teaspoon crushed ginger

2 garlic cloves, crushed

½–1 teaspoon black pepper

1 teaspoon ground cinnamon

1 teaspoon ground turmeric

3 teaspoons paprika

1 teaspoon red chili powder

TO GARNISH

1 cup cilantro leaves, finely chopped

1 tablespoon slivered almonds

CARBOHYDRATE 19 g

FAT 16 g

PROTEIN 25 g

ENERGY 320 kcal/1340 kJ

1 Make the beef stock. When the stock has simmered for 2½ hours or so, make the marinade by mixing together all the ingredients. Add the cubed lamb and mix well. Leave the meat to marinate for 1 hour, or longer, if liked.

2 Heat the oil in a large, heavy pan with a lid. Add the lamb with the marinade and brown over a medium heat. Stir in the onion and cook for about 5 minutes. Add the tomatoes and the hot beef stock and cook gently for 5–10 minutes.

3 Stir in the remaining ingredients, cover, and simmer, stirring occasionally, for 1–1½ hours until the lamb is tender and the liquid has reduced.

4 Garnish with cilantro, and flaked almonds and serve with couscous, if liked.

Nutrition note

Prunes add valuable fiber to this delicious and exotic dish.

PAN-FRIED CHICKEN LIVERS
with fennel

Preparation time: 5 minutes

Cooking time: 10–12 minutes

Serves 4

1 tablespoon all-purpose flour

7½ oz chicken livers

2 teaspoons olive oil

7½-oz fennel bulb with leaves, sliced

3 tablespoons chopped flat-leaf parsley

2 tablespoons lemon juice

salt and black pepper

watercress leaves, to serve

CARBOHYDRATE 6 g

FAT 5 g

PROTEIN 12 g

ENERGY 115 kcal/483 kJ

1 Mix the flour with a little salt and black pepper and use the seasoned flour to coat the chicken livers.

2 Heat the oil in a large skillet and stir-fry the fennel over a moderately high heat for 3 minutes.

3 Add the seasoned liver to the skillet and cook, stirring gently, over a high heat for 5–8 minutes.

4 Slowly mix in the parsley. Pour in the lemon juice, which will make a sizzling sound, remove from the heat, and serve on a bed of watercress.

Nutrition note

Liver is rich in iron and vitamin B_{12}, a vitamin that plays an essential role in the body's ability to produce red blood cells.

GINGER-SPICED TURKEY ESCALOPES
with cashew-nut chutney

Preparation time: 8 minutes

Cooking times: 12–15 minutes

Serves 4

2 tablespoons all-purpose flour

1 teaspoon crushed ginger

1 teaspoon finely chopped tarragon

1 teaspoon dried mixed herbs

4 skinless turkey breasts, about 6 oz each

1 tablespoon corn or canola oil

salt and black pepper

CASHEW-NUT CHUTNEY

½ cup unsalted cashew nuts, coarsely ground

3 tablespoons basil leaves, chopped

1 red onion, finely diced

½ teaspoon red chili powder

½ teaspoon curry powder

juice of 1 lime

juice of 1 orange

black pepper

CARBOHYDRATE 13 g

FAT 14 g

PROTEIN 42 g

ENERGY 344 kcal/1447 kJ

1 Mix the flour with the ginger, tarragon, and mixed herbs and season with salt and black pepper. Use this mixture to coat both sides of each turkey breast.

2 Heat the oil in a nonstick grill pan. Cook the turkey over a medium heat for 12–15 minutes until fully cooked, turning once only to achieve a decorative ridged effect.

3 Meanwhile, make the cashew-nut chutney by mixing together all the ingredients.

4 Serve the turkey breasts immediately accompanied by the cashew-nut chutney.

Nutrition notes

Turkey is naturally low in fat.

Cashew nuts are rich in fat, but remember that this is the healthy monounsaturated type.

SERIOUSLY HOT JERK CHICKEN
with sweet-potato wedges

Preparation time: 20 minutes

Cooking time: 50 minutes

Serves 4

4 skinless chicken breast fillets, about 1 lb in total

JERK SEASONING

8–10 allspice berries

2 scallions, green part only, sliced

4 garlic cloves, crushed

½-inch piece ginger root, peeled and shredded

pinch of finely grated nutmeg

2 pinches of ground cinnamon

1 teaspoon thyme leaves

1–2 Scotch Bonnet chilies, seeded and finely chopped

2 tablespoons reduced-salt soy sauce

juice of 2 limes

SWEET-POTATO WEDGES

2 orange-fleshed sweet potatoes, about 1½ lb in total, unpeeled

1 tablespoon olive oil

2 tablespoons chopped parsley

2 tablespoons chopped chives

CARBOHYDRATE 40 g

FAT 7 g

PROTEIN 31 g

ENERGY 343 kcal/1452 kJ

1 Make the jerk seasoning. Crush the allspice berries using a mortar and pestle or a blender. Add the scallions and pound until well mixed. Add the garlic, ginger, nutmeg, cinnamon, thyme leaves, and chilies. Stir in the soy sauce and lime juice and mix well. If necessary, add a little water to bind.

2 Score the chicken breasts on both sides and rub in the seasoning. Bake the chicken in a preheated 375°F oven for 30–40 minutes until it is crusty on the outside.

3 Meanwhile, put the sweet potatoes in cold water and bring to a boil. Cook the potatoes for 8–10 minutes until parboiled, drain and leave to cool. Remove the skins and cut into wedges.

4 Heat the oil in a nonstick skillet and fry the sweet-potato wedges for about 10 minutes until they are colored on both sides. Sprinkle with the parsley and chives and serve with the cooked chicken cut into thick slices.

Nutrition note

To remove excess fat from the sweet-potato wedges, pat them dry on paper towels before sprinkling with the fresh herbs.

PEANUT AND CHICKEN CASSOULET

Preparation time: 35–40 minutes

Cooking time: 3½ hours

Serves 4

1 teaspoon vegetable oil

1 onion, chopped

1 garlic clove, crushed

1 green bell pepper, cored, seeded, and diced

1 lb chicken breast fillets, each fillet divided into 3 small pieces or fingers

2 heaping tablespoons peanut butter

scant ½ cup unsalted peanuts, skins removed and crushed

1 tablespoon ground coriander seeds

1 teaspoon ground cumin

1 teaspoon red chili powder

2 tomatoes, roughly chopped

1 cup cooked or canned and drained chickpeas

2 tablespoons chopped cilantro leaves, to garnish

CHICKEN STOCK

1 cooked chicken carcass

raw giblets and trimmings (optional)

1 onion, chopped

2–3 carrots, chopped

1 celery stalk, chopped

1 bay leaf

3–4 parsley stalks

1 thyme sprig

7½ cups water

CARBOHYDRATE 20 g

FAT 24 g

PROTEIN 41 g

ENERGY 460 kcal/1920 kJ

1 Make the chicken stock. Chop the chicken carcass into 3–4 pieces and put them in a large saucepan with the rest of the ingredients. Bring to a boil, removing any scum that rises to the surface. Lower the heat and simmer for 2–2½ hours. Strain the stock through a muslin-lined sieve, return to the saucepan and keep warm. These ingredients will make a little more than 4 cups; any stock not used in this recipe can be chilled then frozen for use in other dishes.

2 Meanwhile, using an ovenproof casserole dish that can go on the stovetop, heat the oil, and fry the onion, garlic, and green bell pepper for 5 minutes until soft. Add the chicken pieces and allow to color for 5 minutes.

3 Mix the peanut butter, crushed peanuts, coriander seeds, cumin, and chili powder in a large bowl with 1¼ cups of the chicken stock. Add the peanut mixture to the chicken and cook for a further 5 minutes.

4 Add the tomatoes, chickpeas, and a further 1¼ cups of the chicken stock and cook, covered, in a preheated 375°F oven for about 25 minutes.

5 Remove the casserole lid and continue to cook for a further 20 minutes before serving sprinkled with chopped cilantro leaves.

Nutrition note

Adding chickpeas to the dish means that you do not require as much meat and also lowers the GI.

POACHED GUINEA FOWL
with blueberry marmalade

Preparation time: 10 minutes
Cooking time: 1½ hours
Serves 4

1 guinea fowl, about 2 lb
2½ cups Chicken Stock (see page 69)
1 bouquet garni
1 cup blueberries

CARBOHYDRATE 3 g
FAT 15 g
PROTEIN 28 g
ENERGY 257 kcal/1072 kJ

1 Put the guinea fowl in a large saucepan with the chicken stock and bouquet garni. Add some water if necessary so that the liquid comes about two-thirds of the way up the bird. Bring to a boil and simmer gently for 1–1¼ hours until the meat is tender.

2 Lift the guinea fowl from the cooking liquid, carefully remove the skin, cover the bird with foil, and keep hot.

3 Put ½ cup of the stock in a small saucepan with the blueberries. Boil together rapidly for 10 minutes until the liquid is reduced but the blueberries are still intact.

4 Carve the guinea fowl by removing the breasts whole and cutting each in half. Remove the legs and cut each in half at the joint. In this way each person receives some breast and some darker meat.

5 Serve the meat with a large tablespoon of blueberry marmalade.

Nutrition notes
Blueberries are bursting with valuable antioxidants. Cooking them in the stock releases their sweetness, so no additional sugar is required.

Serve this dish with some low-GI vegetables, such as asparagus or steamed broccoli, to lower the GI even further.

VENISON CASSEROLE

Preparation time: 15 minutes
Cooking time: 2 hours
Serves 4

2 onions, sliced
4 venison steaks, about 4 oz each
1 bouquet garni
½ cinnamon stick
5 pickled walnuts, sliced
1 cup Beef Stock (see page 74)
3 tablespoons red wine
1 teaspoon Angostura bitters
4 large portobello mushrooms
2 tablespoons chopped parsley

CARBOHYDRATE 6 g
FAT 7 g
PROTEIN 30 g
ENERGY 225 kcal/946 kJ

1 Place the onions in a casserole dish and lay the venison steaks on top. Add the bouquet garni, cinnamon stick, and sliced pickled walnuts. Pour over the beef stock, wine, and Angostura bitters and cover. Cook in a preheated 350°F oven for 1¾ hours until the steaks are tender.

2 Remove the stalks from the mushrooms and wipe the caps clean. Add the mushroom caps, whole, to the casserole dish, covering them partially with the juices. Return the casserole to the oven for a further 15 minutes.

3 To serve, place a mushroom on each plate and top with a venison steak. Spoon the meat juices and onions on top and sprinkle with chopped parsley.

Nutrition notes
Venison is an extremely lean meat, which is great for low-fat diets. The delicious sauce in this recipe prevents it from drying out or becoming tough.

Boiled new potatoes and a steamed green vegetable, such as cabbage, are ideal accompaniments to this dish.

ROAST PHEASANT
with cabbage and apple rings

Preparation time: 20 minutes

Cooking time: 50 minutes

Serves 4

2 tablespoons vegetable oil

2 pheasants

3½ oz pancetta, cut into matchsticks

2 garlic cloves, thinly sliced

⅔ cup red wine

1 small Savoy cabbage, about 1 lb, quartered, hard inner stalk removed

1¼ cups Chicken Stock (see page 69)

APPLE RINGS

2 dessert apples, about 9 oz in total, unpeeled, cored, and cut into rings ½ inch thick

2 teaspoons vegetable oil

CARBOHYDRATE 13 g

FAT 29 g

PROTEIN 59 g

ENERGY 570 kcal/2385 kJ

1 Heat the oil in an nonstick roasting pan on the stovetop and brown the pheasants well on all sides over a medium-high heat for about 10 minutes.

2 Roast the pheasants, uncovered and breast-side down, in a preheated 450°F oven for 20 minutes. Remove the pheasants from the pan and set aside for 5 minutes.

3 Place the pancetta in the roasting pan and fry for 2–3 minutes on the stovetop until brown. Add the garlic and cook for 1 minute. Pour in the wine and boil to reduce. Separate the cabbage into leaves and add to the pan along with the stock.

4 Use poultry shears or a carving knife to cut the pheasants in half through the breastbone. Return the pheasant halves to the pancetta and cabbage mixture. Cover with foil and cook gently over a low heat on the stovetop for 15 minutes.

5 Meanwhile, make the apple rings. Heat the oil in a nonstick skillet and fry the apple rings for about 5 minutes until they are brown on each side.

6 Serve the pheasant halves on a bed of the cabbage mixture, with the juices as a gravy and decorated with the apple rings.

Nutrition notes

Savoy cabbage is rich in betacarotene, an antioxidant that helps prevent cell damage by free radicals.

The pancetta contains plenty of salt, so no additional salt is needed in this recipe.

BRAISED OXTAIL
with orange

Preparation time: 30 minutes

Cooking time: 3 hours, plus making the stock

Serves 4

1 teaspoon vegetable oil

2 onions, sliced

1 oxtail, about 2 lb, cut into pieces and trimmed of as much fat as possible

12 oz carrots, sliced

1¼-lb yellow rutabaga, chopped into 4 large pieces

1 bouquet garni

1 tablespoon tomato paste

3 oranges, peeled, pith removed, and sliced

BEEF STOCK

1½ lb lean beef shank, cubed

2 onions, chopped

2–3 carrots, chopped

1 bay leaf

1 bouquet garni

4–6 peppercorns

6 cups water

½ teaspoon salt

TO GARNISH

2 tablespoons chopped parsley

grated zest of 1 orange

CARBOHYDRATE 32 g

FAT 14 g

PROTEIN 32 g

ENERGY 376 kcal/1576 kJ

1 Make the beef stock. Put all the ingredients in a large saucepan. Bring to a boil slowly then immediately reduce the heat to a slow simmer. Cover the pan with a well-fitting lid and simmer for 4 hours, removing any scum that rises to the surface. Remove from the heat and strain the stock through a muslin-lined sieve and leave to cool before refrigerating. These ingredients will make about 5 cups. Any stock that is not used can be chilled then frozen for use in other recipes.

2 Meanwhile, heat the oil in a large, Dutch oven on the stovetop. Add the onion to soften for 4–5 minutes.

3 Add the pieces of oxtail to the pan. Cook for 5 minutes until brown on all sides.

4 Add the carrot and rutabaga to the pan and cook until they are lightly browned. Gradually stir in 2 cups of the stock and then add the bouquet garni, tomato paste, and orange rounds. Heat the mixture to simmering.

5 Cover and cook in a preheated 300°F oven for 2½–3 hours until the oxtail is tender. Remove the bouquet garni.

6 Serve the oxtail, garnished with chopped parsley and grated orange zest, together with the vegetables and sauce.

Nutrition notes

Keep the rutabaga in as large pieces as possible and avoid mashing it, because this raises the GI.

Including both carrots and rutabaga in the dish instead of potato means that it is easy to eat more of your recommended daily vegetable portions.

LOIN OF PORK
with artichoke hearts

Preparation time: 25 minutes

Cooking time: 1 hour 20 minutes

Serves 4

2 teaspoons olive oil

1¼ lb boneless rolled top loin of pork

¼ cup dry white wine

½ cup Vegetable Stock (see page 14)

2 large onions, sliced into thin rounds

4 tomatoes, skinned (see page 43) and quartered

14-oz can artichoke hearts, drained and quartered

2 teaspoons coriander seeds, lightly crushed

salt

TO SERVE

2 tablespoons chopped parsley

1½ cups basmati rice

CARBOHYDRATE 71 g

FAT 14 g

PROTEIN 41 g

ENERGY 565 kcal/2374 kJ

1 Heat the oil in an ovenproof casserole dish that can go on the stovetop, and cook the pork gently for about 10 minutes, turning it halfway so that it is evenly browned.

2 Add the wine and vegetable stock and bring to a boil before reducing the heat to a gentle simmer. Cover and cook in a preheated 375°F oven for around 40–50 minutes.

3 Remove the meat, cover it with foil, and set aside. Return the casserole dish to the stovetop and bring the juices to a boil until they thicken slightly. (If few juices remain, add a little more vegetable stock to remove the flavors from the pan.)

4 Add the onions to the juices and cook until softened. Stir in the tomatoes, artichoke hearts, and coriander seeds. Cover and cook on a medium-low heat for 8–10 minutes until the tomatoes soften.

5 Meanwhile, cook the basmati rice in lightly salted boiling water for 12–15 minutes or according to package instructions.

6 Slice the pork and serve it, sprinkled with chopped parsley, with the artichoke hearts, tomato and onion mixture, and basmati rice.

Nutrition note
Trimmed pork loin is a lean cut of meat and consequently lower in fat. Serve with basmati rice, one of the varieties with the lowest GI.

SIRLOIN STEAK
with crunchy horseradish cream

Preparation time: 5 minutes

Cooking time: 2–12 minutes

Serves 4

1 teaspoon vegetable oil

sirloin steak, about 1 lb in total

shredded lettuce leaves, to serve

HORSERADISH CREAM

¾ cup low-fat plain, strained yogurt

⅔ cup shelled walnuts, chopped

¼ cup horseradish sauce

CARBOHYDRATE 37 g

FAT 20 g

PROTEIN 30 g

ENERGY 322 kcal/1342 kJ

1 Make the horseradish cream. Mix together the yogurt, chopped walnuts, and horseradish.

2 Heat a grill pan until it is hot and brush the surface with the oil.

3 Put the steaks on the grill and cook, turning once only to achieve a decorative ridged effect. The following timing is a rough guide for steaks that are about 1 inch thick. Blue: 1–2 minutes each side (soft to touch with no feel of resistance); rare: 2–3 minutes each side (soft and spongy, may still ooze some red meat juices when pressed); medium rare: 3–4 minutes each side (a little firmer); medium: 4–5 minutes each side (firm to touch); well done: more than 5 minutes each side (solid).

4 Serve the steaks accompanied by the horseradish cream and shredded lettuce leaves.

Nutrition note

Walnuts are a great source of protein and healthy omega-3 fats.

CITRUS ROAST DUCK
on wilted spinach leaves

Preparation time: 20 minutes

Cooking time: 1½ hours

Serves 4

1 duck, about 4 lb with giblets, giblets removed and duck washed and dried with paper towels

1 tablespoon unsalted butter

2 shallots, finely sliced

8⅓ cups baby spinach leaves

1 tablespoon thyme leaves

sea salt

black pepper

mandarin-orange segments, to garnish

CITRUS SAUCE

3 mandarin oranges

scant ¼ cup port

1¼ cups Chicken Stock (see page 69)

lemon juice, to taste

CARBOHYDRATE 8 g

FAT 14 g

PROTEIN 29 g

ENERGY 282 kcal/1180 kJ

1 Either put a roasting rack in an oven tray or line an oven tray with crumpled foil so that the fat can drain from the duck during roasting.

2 Prick the duck all over with a skewer and put it on the rack or foil in the oven tray. Season well with sea salt and black pepper and roast the duck in a preheated 450°F oven for 1–1½ hours, draining the fat frequently during cooking. Do not baste. Check that the juices run clear at the end of the cooking time by inserting a skewer into the fattest part of a leg.

3 Meanwhile, make the citrus sauce. Grate the zest from the mandarin oranges. Peel the mandarin oranges, remove the pith and pips, and liquidize the flesh until smooth. Mix together the mandarin pulp, zest, port, and stock in a saucepan and boil until the sauce thickens slightly. Stir in lemon juice to taste.

4 Melt the butter in a large skillet and pan-fry the shallots until softened. Add the spinach and thyme and cook until the leaves have wilted.

5 Serve the spinach leaves on a warm plate, lay the cooked duck on top, and coat with the citrus sauce. Garnish with mandarin-orange segments.

Nutrition note
Duck is very high in fat, but cooking in this way allows some of the fat to drain away. Do not use the juices for gravy because they are rich in saturated fat, which is less healthy.

PAN-FRIED CALVES' LIVER
with pears

Preparation time: 15 minutes, plus marinating and soaking

Cooking time: 4–5 minutes

Serves 4

2 large Comice pears, unpeeled, quartered, cored, and thinly sliced

1 teaspoon balsamic vinegar

12 oz calves' liver, sliced thinly

3 tablespoons skim milk

2½ cups wild arugula leaves

3 cups baby spinach leaves

⅓ cup pecan nuts, chopped

1 teaspoon vegetable oil

DRESSING

2 teaspoons balsamic vinegar

1 teaspoon chili-infused olive oil

CARBOHYDRATE 16 g

FAT 16 g

PROTEIN 22 g

ENERGY 290 kcal/1214 kJ

1 Place the pear slices in a dish, sprinkle over the balsamic vinegar, and leave to marinate.

2 Put the calves' liver in a flat dish and pour over the milk, then soak for 30 minutes to remove any bitterness.

3 Meanwhile, mix the dressing ingredients together. Toss the arugula and baby spinach leaves in the dressing. Arrange the leaves on individual plates and arrange slices of marinated pear on top. Sprinkle over the chopped pecans.

4 Discard the milk and pat the liver dry on paper towels. Heat the oil in a nonstick skillet and pan-fry the liver for about 2 minutes on each side (depending on the thickness of the liver) until it is brown.

5 Serve the hot liver on top of the dressed salad.

Nutrition note

Serving a good helping of salad greens and nuts alongside the liver lowers the GI of the meal as well as providing important antioxidant vitamins and minerals.

Vegetarian
Creations

GARLIC, ROASTED BELL PEPPER, AND WALNUT PAPPARDELLE

Preparation time: 10–15 minutes

Cooking time: 35 minutes

Serves 4

2 teaspoons olive oil

4 red bell peppers, cored, seeded, and sliced

3–4 large garlic cloves, thinly sliced

½ cup walnuts, chopped

10 oz fresh egg pappardelle

⅓ cup Parmesan cheese shavings

salt and black pepper

CARBOHYDRATE 63 g

FAT 16 g

PROTEIN 15 g

ENERGY 435 kcal/1833 kJ

1 Brush ½ teaspoon of the olive oil over the bell peppers. Put the bell peppers on a baking pan and roast them in a preheated 230°C oven for 20–25 minutes until they are soft and beginning to blacken.

2 Reserve 4 slices of bell pepper to use as a garnish and cut the remaining bell peppers into large dice.

3 Heat the remaining olive oil in a large skillet over a medium-low heat, add the sliced garlic but do not let it brown. Add the diced red bell pepper and stir in the walnuts. Keep warm.

4 Bring a large saucepan of lightly salted water to the boil. Add the pasta, return to a boil, and cook for 3–4 minutes or until the pasta is *al dente*. Drain and transfer to a large, warm serving bowl.

5 Toss the pasta well with the garlic, bell pepper, and walnut mixture. Sprinkle over the Parmesan shavings, and serve immediately, garnished with the reserved bell pepper slices.

Nutrition note

Walnuts contain healthy monounsaturated fats and a range of vitamins and minerals. Teaming them with fresh egg pasta, which can be lower in GI than normal pasta, makes a winning combination.

RUSTIC PASTA

Preparation time: 20 minutes

Cooking time: 20 minutes

Serves 4

1 lb broccoli, cut into florets

2 teaspoons olive oil

1 large onion, finely chopped

1 garlic clove, crushed

3 medium tomatoes, skinned (see page 43), and chopped

1 tablespoon tomato paste

1 cup pitted black olives in herb-flavored brine, drained

2 tablespoons chopped thyme

10 oz dried whole-wheat pasta shapes, such as fusilli

6 Darjeeling teabags

1 cup low-fat buffalo mozzarella cheese, torn into small pieces

black pepper

TO SERVE

4 tomatoes, sliced

handful of basil leaves, torn

2 tablespoons balsamic vinegar

CARBOHYDRATE 64 g

FAT 12 g

PROTEIN 25 g

ENERGY 446 kcal/1883 kJ

1 Cook the broccoli florets in boiling water for about 3 minutes until just tender. Drain.

2 Meanwhile, heat the oil in a large skillet and gently cook the onion and garlic until they are soft.

3 Add the tomatoes, tomato paste, olives, broccoli, and thyme and cook for about 3 minutes. Season with black pepper and keep warm.

4 Bring a large saucepan of lightly salted water to a boil. Add the pasta and teabags, return to a boil, and cook for 8–10 minutes or until the pasta is *al dente*. Discard the teabags and drain the pasta.

5 Toss the pasta in the broccoli sauce and add the chunks of torn mozzarella. Serve immediately in warm bowls with the sliced tomatoes and basil leaves and drizzled with balsamic vinegar.

Nutrition notes

Whole-wheat pasta retains its beneficial fiber when cooked.

The broccoli and olives enhance the nutritional value of this dish.

PENNE
with olives and sun-dried tomatoes

Preparation time: 10 minutes
Cooking time: 8–12 minutes
Serves 4

8 oz dried penne
1 cup peas
1 tablespoon olive oil
2 garlic cloves, crushed
4 shallots, finely chopped
1 green bell pepper, cored, seeded, and diced
3 tablespoons chopped mint
⅓ cup basil leaves, chopped
4 oz sun-dried tomatoes in oil, drained and sliced
½ cup pitted black olives
1 tablespoon capers, chopped
⅔ cup low-fat crème fraîche
salt and black pepper

CARBOHYDRATE 56 g
FAT 28 g
PROTEIN 14 g
ENERGY 515 kcal/2156 kJ

1 Bring a large pan of lightly salted water to a boil. Add the pasta, return to a boil, and cook for 8–10 minutes or until the pasta is *al dente*.

2 Meanwhile, cook the peas in lightly salted boiling water for 5 minutes.

3 Heat the oil in a large nonstick skillet. Add the garlic, shallots, bell pepper, and peas and fry for about 5 minutes until the onions are light brown and the peppers are just cooked.

4 Drain the pasta. Add the herbs, tomatoes, olives, capers, and cooked pasta to the skillet. Season to taste. Heat through, stir in the crème fraîche and serve immediately.

Nutrition note
Pasta is an excellent low-GI food to use as the basis of meals because it is absorbed slowly by the body, which makes it very sustaining.

GARLIC LINGUINI
and wild porcini

Preparation time: 15–20 minutes, plus soaking

Cooking time: 5–10 minutes

Serves 2

½ cup dried porcini mushrooms

8 oz fresh linguini

2 tablespoons olive oil

4 shallots, sliced

4 garlic cloves, thinly sliced

2 carrots, grated

1 heaped teaspoon dried oregano

3⅓ cups cilantro leaves and stems, chopped

1 garlic clove, crushed

scant ½ cup finely grated Parmesan cheese

2 teaspoons extra virgin olive oil, to serve

oregano leaves, to garnish

CARBOHYDRATE 114 g

FAT 24 g

PROTEIN 26 g

ENERGY 743 kcal/3127 kJ

1 Soak the mushrooms in a bowl of warm water for 30 minutes. Drain and reserve the mushroom liquor.

2 Make the mushroom liquor up to about 6¼ cups with water, transfer to a large pan, and bring to a boil. Add the pasta, return to a boil, and cook for 2 minutes or until the pasta is *al dente*.

3 Heat the oil in a large, deep nonstick skillet and fry the shallots and sliced garlic for a few minutes.

4 Add the soaked mushrooms, carrots, dried oregano, and cilantro and stir-fry for 1–2 minutes. Add a few tablespoons of hot water if the mixture begins to stick to the bottom of the skillet.

5 Drain the pasta and stir it into the vegetable mixture with the crushed garlic and half the Parmesan. Heat through and serve drizzled with extra virgin olive oil and sprinkled with the remaining Parmesan cheese and the oregano leaves.

Nutrition notes

Grating a strong cheese such as Parmesan will encourage you to use less and therefore keep down your intake of saturated fat.

Garlic has been shown to help thin the blood and hence protect against heart disease.

INDIVIDUAL DHAL SOUFFLÉS

Preparation time: 15 minutes

Cooking time: 1¼ hours

Serves 4

1 heaping tablespoon butter

¼ cup all-purpose flour

2½ cups skim milk

yolks of 2 large eggs

whites of 4 large eggs

2 tablespoons chopped chives

1 teaspoon vegetable oil

green salad, to serve

SPICED DHAL

1 teaspoon cumin seeds

1⅛ cups moong dhal, washed until water runs clear

1 small onion, sliced

2 cinnamon sticks

1 small chili, seeded and chopped

salt and black pepper

CARBOHYDRATE 48 g

FAT 9 g

PROTEIN 24 g

ENERGY 365 kcal/1527 kJ

1 Make the spiced dhal. Toast the cumin seeds in a dry skillet over medium heat until they start to pop. Put the moong dhal in a saucepan and add sufficient water to cover, bring to a boil, and simmer rapidly for 15 minutes. Drain the dhal, rinsing in hot water.

2 Return the dhal to the saucepan with the onion and cinnamon sticks. Add sufficient hot water to cover the dhal by about ½ inch. Bring back to a boil, reduce the heat, and simmer gently for 25–30 minutes. Drain off any excess liquid and discard the cinnamon sticks. Add the chili, a pinch of salt, a liberal amount of black pepper, and the toasted cumin seeds. Mix well.

3 Melt the butter in a saucepan and stir in the flour. Cook, stirring, for 1–2 minutes. Meanwhile, warm the milk in a separate saucepan. Remove the butter and flour mixture from the heat and whisk in the warm milk until the sauce is smooth. Return to the heat and continue whisking until the sauce thickens.

4 Mix the white sauce into the spiced dhal and stir in the egg yolks.

5 Beat the egg whites in a large bowl until firm and gently stir one-third into the spiced mixture. Fold in the remainder of the egg whites with a metal spoon. Mix in the chives.

6 Lightly grease 4 ramekin dishes with the oil. Pour the egg and dhal mixture into the ramekins and cook in a preheated 375°F oven for 15–20 minutes until they begin to brown and are firm to the touch. Serve immediately with a green salad.

Nutrition note

Legumes are a great source of soluble fiber and keep the GI of a meal low. This is especially true of this recipe as the lentils (moong dhal) are not pureed.

ALMOND AND APRICOT WILD RICE
with cumin seeds

Preparation time: 20 minutes, plus soaking

Cooking time: 20 minutes

Serves 4

2 cups long grain and wild rice

2 tablespoons olive oil

3 shallots, quartered

2 garlic cloves, crushed

2 teaspoons cumin seeds

4 red and 4 black peppercorns

⅓ cup whole almonds, toasted

10-oz can borlotti beans, drained

⅓ cup dried apricots, roughly chopped

½ teaspoon ground turmeric

3½ cups Vegetable Stock, lightly salted (see page 14)

4 scallions, green stems only, sliced

2 heaping tablespoons roughly chopped mint

salt and black pepper

TO SERVE

2 tablespoons lemon juice

¼ cup grated Parmesan cheese

1–2 teaspoons red chili powder (optional)

1 cup less 2 tablespoons low-fat plain, strained yogurt

CARBOHYDRATE 120 g

FAT 17 g

PROTEIN 16 g

ENERGY 538 kcal/2270 kJ

1 Wash and soak the rice in a bowl of cold water while you prepare the other ingredients.

2 Heat the oil in a large, heavy skillet with a lid. Fry the shallots and garlic for 1–2 minutes, then add the cumin seeds and peppercorns and stir-fry for a few seconds.

3 Chop half the almonds, reserving the rest for garnish. Add the chopped almonds, beans, apricots, turmeric, and stock to the pan and stir thoroughly.

4 Stir in the drained rice, cover, and simmer for 15 minutes. Add the scallions and mint, check the seasoning, and stir gently. Add a little hot water if the pan is dry and the rice is not fully cooked. Allow to cook, covered, for a further 3 minutes.

5 Serve with a drizzle of lemon juice, a sprinkling of Parmesan cheese, the remaining almonds, and chili powder, if using. Offer the yogurt separately.

Nutrition notes

Different types of rice have different GI values. Risotto rice tends to have the highest GI, so try not to use it too often.

The beans, apricots, lemon, and almonds in this recipe will help to keep the GI low.

PEA AND MINT FRITTATA

Preparation time: 20 minutes

Cooking time: 10 minutes

Serves 4

7 oz sweet potato, sliced

⅔ cup peas

1 tablespoon olive oil

2 shallots, finely sliced

1 red bell pepper, cored, seeded, and thinly sliced lengthwise

6 eggs, beaten

1 tablespoon skim milk

1 tablespoon freshly grated Parmesan cheese

4 tablespoons chopped mint

frisée lettuce leaves, to serve

black pepper

CARBOHYDRATE 16 g

FAT 13 g

PROTEIN 14 g

ENERGY 235 kcal/980 kJ

1 Cook the sweet potato and peas in a saucepan of boiling water for 4–5 minutes until tender. Drain.

2 Heat the oil in a deep, nonstick skillet and stir-fry the shallots and red bell pepper over a moderate heat for 1–2 minutes. Stir in the peas and sweet potatoes and warm through for a further 2 minutes.

3 Combine the eggs with the milk and Parmesan and season to taste with black pepper. Pour the egg mixture over the vegetables, lifting the vegetables slightly so that the egg runs to the bottom of the pan. Cook gently over a low heat and lightly stir in the mint.

4 Preheat the broiler to medium-hot and cook the top of the frittata for 3–4 minutes until it is brown and fluffy. Remove, cut into wedges, and serve with a grind of black pepper and accompanied by frisée lettuce leaves.

Nutrition notes

The Parmesan in this recipe provides a salty flavor, so you don't need to add extra salt.

Using vegetables that are different colors helps provide a varied range of nutrients: betacarotene from the sweet potato and B vitamins and vitamin C from the peas. Weight for weight, the red bell peppers contain three times as much vitamin C as an orange.

SPEEDY KIDNEY BEAN AND CILANTRO CURRY

Preparation time: 5 minutes

Cooking time: 5 minutes

Serves 4

2 teaspoons corn oil

1 teaspoon cumin seeds

1 tablespoon tomato paste

2 teaspoons curry powder

1 teaspoon ground turmeric

1 teaspoon ground coriander seeds

1 teaspoon ground cumin

2 teaspoons garam masala

13¼-oz can kidney beans, drained

2 scallions, sliced

2 tablespoons chopped cilantro leaves

salt

mixed salad greens or pitta breads, to serve

CARBOHYDRATE 21 g

FAT 3 g

PROTEIN 8 g

ENERGY 136 kcal/572 kJ

1 Heat the oil in a nonstick pan. Add the cumin seeds and let them pop for a few seconds.

2 Stir in the tomato paste, curry powder, ground spices, and garam masala and blend well together over a low heat.

3 Mix in the kidney beans, scallions and cilantro leaves. Add salt to taste and stir in a few tablespoons of hot water if you prefer more sauce. Serve hot with mixed salad greens or in pitta breads.

Nutrition note

Beans and lentils are high in soluble fiber, which helps control blood-glucose levels. This type of fiber has also been shown to lower blood fats, such as cholesterol. Try to eat two large helpings of beans or lentils every day.

SPICY SCRAMBLED EGG
with onion and red bell pepper

Preparation time: 5 minutes

Cooking time: 5–10 minutes

Serves 4

1 tablespoon olive oil

1 tablespoon sesame oil

1 large onion, sliced

1 red bell pepper, cored, seeded, and sliced

1 teaspoon cumin seeds

1 teaspoon crushed ginger

8 eggs

2 tablespoons water

salt and black pepper

TO SERVE

2 whole-wheat pitta breads

2 tablespoons sweet chili dipping sauce

10 chive stalks, snipped

CARBOHYDRATE 21 g

FAT 18 g

PROTEIN 19 g

ENERGY 320 kcal/1344 kJ

1 Heat the oils in a skillet and fry the onion and bell pepper for 2–3 minutes over a moderate heat until they are soft but not browned. Stir in the cumin seeds and ginger and fry for 1 minute

2 Beat the eggs and the measurement water and season to taste. Add the eggs to the skillet and stir-fry for about 2 minutes until lightly scrambled and just cooked.

3 Meanwhile, toast the pitta breads, then cut into diagonal strips and serve with the spicy scrambled egg. Drizzle the dipping sauce around the outside and garnish with snipped chives.

Nutrition note

Although eggs contain cholesterol, dietary cholesterol does not have a significant effect on blood cholesterol. So, unless you have been advised otherwise, it is fine to have about five eggs each week as part of an overall balanced diet.

MEDITERRANEAN BELL PEPPERS

Preparation time: 10 minutes

Cooking time: 1 hour

Serves 4

2 red and 2 yellow bell peppers, halved, cored, and seeded but stems left intact

24 cherry tomatoes, halved

2 garlic cloves, thinly sliced

1½ tablespoons capers in brine, drained and rinsed

1 bunch basil

2 tablespoons olive oil

black pepper

mixed salad greens, to serve

CARBOHYDRATE 10 g

FAT 8 g

PROTEIN 5 g

ENERGY 128 kcal/535 kJ

1 Place the mixed bell peppers, cut-side up, in a shallow baking dish.

2 Divide the halved cherry tomatoes, slivers of garlic, and capers between the pepper halves. Add a few basil leaves then lightly drizzle each pepper with olive oil and season with black pepper.

3 Pour 1¼ cups water into the base of the dish to prevent the bell peppers from sticking. Cover tightly with foil and cook in a preheated 350°F oven for 20 minutes. Remove the foil, reduce the temperature to 300°F, and bake for another 40 minutes until soft.

4 Garnish the peppers with the remaining basil leaves and serve with mixed salad greens.

Nutrition notes

Red and yellow bell peppers are rich in betacarotene, which is converted to the antioxidant vitamin A in the body.

Olive oil, an integral part of the Mediterranean diet, is high in unsaturated fats, which are beneficial for your heart.

RED LENTIL DHAL
with cucumber raita

Preparation time: 15 minutes

Cooking time: 30 minutes

Serves 4

1⅛ cups red lentils

1 tablespoon canola oil

1 large onion, finely chopped

2 garlic cloves, crushed

1 teaspoon crushed ginger

2 green chilies, seeded and finely chopped

4 tomatoes, finely chopped

½ teaspoon ground turmeric

1½ teaspoons garam masala

2 cups hot water

4 tablespoons lemon juice

3⅓ cups cilantro leaves and stems, chopped

salt

pitta breads, to serve

RAITA

4-inch piece of cucumber, grated

2 cups low-fat plain yogurt

1 teaspoon cumin seeds

½ teaspoon black pepper

TO GARNISH

3 scallions, green stems only, sliced diagonally

½ teaspoon red chili powder

CARBOHYDRATE 48 g

FAT 5 g

PROTEIN 22 g

ENERGY 316 kcal/1336 kJ

1 Soak the lentils in a bowl of warm water. Heat the oil in a large, nonstick skillet with a lid. Stir-fry the onion, garlic, ginger, and chilies for 3–5 minutes. Stir in the tomatoes and cook, stirring occasionally, until the tomatoes begin to go mushy. Add the turmeric and garam masala. Cover and simmer, stirring occasionally, for 5 minutes.

2 Drain the lentils and add them, along with the measurement water to the skillet. Stir well, cover, and cook for 15–20 minutes until the dhal is tender but not mushy. Add a little more water if the dhal is too dry.

3 Meanwhile, make the raita. Drain the grated cucumber on paper towels and add this to the other ingredients. Chill until ready to serve.

4 When the dhal is cooked, gently stir in salt to taste, lemon juice, and cilantro. Garnish with the scallions and sprinkle red chili powder over the raita. Serve with pitta breads.

Nutrition notes

This dish is a good source of soluble fiber and lycopene.

Vegetarian meals can often be low in iron; the garam masala in this recipe will provide some iron, and combining it with the vitamin C from the fresh cilantro and lime juice will enhance the rate at which it is absorbed.

QUORN™ AND CASHEW STIR-FRY

Preparation time: 10 minutes

Cooking time: 20 minutes

Serves 4

2 tablespoons canola oil

1 onion, sliced lengthwise

2 teaspoons crushed ginger

⅔ cup cashew nuts

4¾ cups snow peas

8 oz Quorn™ pieces

2 tablespoons soy sauce

1½ cups mixed oyster and shiitake mushrooms

2 teaspoons five spice powder

8 oz baby sweetcorn

3 cups bok choy, shredded

4 scallions, sliced diagonally

1 teaspoon black pepper

2 tablespoons chopped flat-leaf parsley

2 tablespoons chopped mint

2 teaspoons sesame seeds, to serve

CARBOHYDRATE 16 g

FAT 21 g

PROTEIN 21 g

ENERGY 334 kcal/1389 kJ

1 Heat the oil in a nonstick wok or large skillet and stir-fry the onion, ginger, cashews, and snow peas for a few minutes.

2 Stir in the Quorn™, soy sauce, mushrooms, and five spice powder. Stir-fry for 7–10 minutes until almost cooked and then add the baby sweetcorn. Stir-fry for 2 minutes more before adding the bok choy. Add a few tablespoons of hot water from time to time to prevent burning.

3 Add the remaining ingredients, cook through, check the seasoning, and serve sprinkled with the sesame seeds.

Nutrition note

Quorn™ is a tasty and low-fat way to enjoy vegetarian meals. It absorbs flavors well and cooks in minutes.

STIR-FRIED NOODLES
with portobello mushrooms

Preparation time: 10 minutes

Cooking time: 10 minutes

Serves 4

7½ oz thread egg noodles

1 tablespoon corn oil

1 large onion, sliced lengthwise

½-inch piece of fresh ginger root, finely chopped

7 oz portobello mushrooms, halved and thickly sliced

1 cup bean sprouts

2 large red bell peppers, cored, seeded, and thinly sliced

1 tablespoon plum sauce

2 tablespoons light soy sauce

6 scallions, sliced diagonally into ¾-inch pieces

CARBOHYDRATE 53 g

FAT 8 g

PROTEIN 11 g

ENERGY 317 kcal/1336 kJ

1 Cook the noodles in a pan of boiling water for 3–4 minutes. Drain, rinse, and set aside.

2 Meanwhile, heat the oil in a wok or large skillet and stir-fry the onion and ginger for 2–3 minutes. Add the mushrooms and cook for 1–2 minutes over a medium heat.

3 Stir in the bean sprouts, bell peppers, plum sauce, soy sauce, and scallions and cook for a further few minutes, stirring occasionally.

4 Mix in the noodles, adjust the seasoning, and heat through before serving.

Nutrition notes
Stir-frying is a quick method of cooking that helps preserve nutrients.

Don't be tempted to add salt—the soy sauce in this recipe makes it salty enough.

BULGUR WHEAT SALAD
with spiced yogurt

Preparation time: 20 minutes, plus soaking and resting

Serves 2

¾ cup bulgur wheat

4 large plums, pitted, and each cut into about 8 slices

1 garlic clove, crushed

1 red onion, finely chopped

½ cup flat-leaf parsley, chopped

handful of mint, chopped

2 tablespoons olive oil

4 tablespoons lemon juice

salt and black pepper

SPICED YOGURT

4 tablespoons low-fat plain yogurt

1 garlic clove, crushed

½ teaspoon cayenne pepper

½ teaspoon tomato paste

finely chopped chives, to garnish

CARBOHYDRATE 38 g

FAT 7 g

PROTEIN 6 g

ENERGY 230 kcal/965 kJ

1 Place the bulgur wheat in a large bowl, cover it with water, and leave for 30 minutes to swell up.

2 Drain away any excess water from the bulgur wheat and squeeze it dry with your hands.

3 Mix in all the other ingredients and put the salad in the refrigerator to rest for at least 30 minutes to allow the flavors to develop.

4 Make the spiced yogurt. Mix together all the ingredients and garnish with finely chopped chives.

5 Serve the bulgur wheat salad accompanied by the spiced yogurt.

Nutrition notes
Bulgur wheat is a great alternative to rice and has a lower GI.

Plums make a refreshing addition to this dish and also help to keep down the GI.

CHICKPEA AND OLIVE SALAD

Preparation time: 10 minutes

Serves 4

8-oz can chickpeas, drained

½ cup pitted black olives, halved

½ red onion, finely chopped

1 cup cherry tomatoes, halved

3 tablespoons chopped flat-leaf parsley, plus extra to garnish

2 cups watercress, to serve

DRESSING

1 garlic clove, crushed

½ cup low-fat plain, strained yogurt

juice of ½ lime

black pepper

CARBOHYDRATE 33 g

FAT 4 g

PROTEIN 7 g

ENERGY 122 kcal/516 kJ

1 Make the dressing. Mix together the garlic, yogurt, and lime juice. Season to taste with black pepper.

2 Stir together the chickpeas, olives, onion, tomatoes, and parsley.

3 Add the dressing to the chickpea mixture, mix thoroughly, and serve on a bed of watercress leaves, garnished with chopped parsley.

Nutrition note

Chickpeas are high in soluble fiber. This type of fiber is thought to help lower blood-cholesterol levels.

Sumptuous
Side Dishes

GINGER BROCCOLI
with fennel seeds

Preparation time: 5 minutes

Cooking time: 5 minutes

Serves 4

2 teaspoons olive oil

1 teaspoon crushed ginger

½ teaspoon fennel seeds

1 lb broccoli, cut into florets

3 tablespoons reduced-salt soy sauce

black pepper, to taste

CARBOHYDRATE 4 g

FAT 3 g

PROTEIN 7 g

ENERGY 64 kcal/267 kJ

1 Heat the oil in a nonstick wok or skillet and stir-fry the ginger and fennel seeds over a medium heat for a few seconds.

2 Add the broccoli, soy sauce, and black pepper and stir-fry until the broccoli is just cooked.

Nutrition note
One serving of this dish provides just over one serving toward the daily fruit and vegetable intake recommended by the U.S. Department of Health and Human Services and Department of Agriculture's (USDA) Dietary Guidelines for Americans.

RED CABBAGE COLESLAW

Preparation time: 10 minutes, plus chilling

Serves 4

7½-oz red cabbage, shredded or grated

4 carrots, grated

3 scallions, sliced

3 tablespoons chopped flat-leaf parsley

2 tablespoons shredded basil leaves

½ cup reduced-calorie mayonnaise

¼ cup low-fat plain yogurt

CARBOHYDRATE 12 g

FAT 8 g

PROTEIN 2 g

ENERGY 125 kcal/520 kJ

1 Mix all the ingredients together. Chill for 20–30 minutes before serving.

Nutrition note

The reduced-calorie mayonnaise used here helps keep the fat content lower than in standard coleslaw, and the low-fat plain yogurt adds creaminess without piling on the fat.

ZUCCHINI RONDELLES

Preparation time: 5 minutes

Cooking time: 10 minutes

Serves 4

1 tablespoon olive oil

pinch of reduced-salt vegetable bouillon powder

2 yellow and 2 green zucchini, thinly sliced into rounds

½ teaspoon crushed dried chilies

2 tablespoons lemon juice

TO GARNISH

16 baby plum tomatoes, cut in half lengthwise

cilantro leaves, chopped

CARBOHYDRATE 5 g

FAT 3 g

PROTEIN 2 g

ENERGY 50 kcal/215 kJ

1 Heat the oil in a large, nonstick skillet. Add the vegetable bouillon powder and stir until well blended.

2 Add the thinly sliced zucchini and sauté over a medium heat for 5–8 minutes until they take on an intense green-yellow color. Do not brown.

3 Season with the crushed dried chilies and lemon juice and serve garnished with the baby plum tomatoes and cilantro leaves.

FRAGRANT CINNAMON BASMATI RICE

Preparation time: 10 minutes, plus soaking

Cooking time: 18–20 minutes

Serves 4

1½ cups basmati rice

4¼ cups water, for soaking

2 cups water, for cooking

1½ cups peas

2 teaspoons cumin seeds

4 sticks cinnamon, each broken into 2–3 pieces

3 black cardamom pods

3 star anise

1 teaspoon salt

1 teaspoon butter

CARBOHYDRATE 60 g

FAT 3 g

PROTEIN 8 g

ENERGY 280 kcal/1195 kJ

1 Wash the rice in several changes of water. Then soak the rice in a large bowl filled with the measurement soaking water for 2 hours.

2 Drain the rice then put it with all the other ingredients into a large pan and pour in the measurement cooking water. Cover with a tight-fitting lid.

3 Cook over a medium heat for 18–20 minutes, stirring gently halfway through cooking.

Nutrition note

Basmati rice has one of the lowest GI ratings of all types of rice.

CARAMELIZED GREEN BEANS

Preparation time: 5 minutes

Cooking time: 12–15 minutes

Serves 2

2 teaspoons olive oil

1 garlic clove, crushed

2 cups (7 oz) fine green beans, topped and tailed

1 tablespoon thyme leaves

3 tablespoons balsamic vinegar

2 tablespoons soy sauce, or salt to taste

¼ teaspoon black pepper

1 teaspoon sesame seeds, to serve

CARBOHYDRATE 5 g

FAT 4 g

PROTEIN 4 g

ENERGY 74 kcal/307 kJ

1 Heat the oil in a nonstick skillet, add the garlic and the beans, and stir-fry over a medium heat for 2–3 minutes.

2 Stir in the thyme leaves, balsamic vinegar, and soy sauce (or salt) and black pepper. Cook for 10–12 minutes, until the beans are just cooked, adding a few tablespoons of hot water if the beans begin to stick to the bottom.

3 Serve sprinkled with the sesame seeds.

Nutrition note

Cooking fresh vegetables quickly, so that they still have some "bite," helps to preserve the nutrients.

SWEET POTATO AND CHILI MASH

Preparation time: 10 minutes

Cooking time: 15 minutes

Serves 4

3 sweet potatoes, about 1¾ lb in total, chopped

1 teaspoon butter

2 tablespoons skim milk

⅓ cup snipped chives

1–2 tablespoons sweet chili sauce

CARBOHYDRATE 47 g

FAT 2 g

PROTEIN 3 g

ENERGY 205 kcal/874 kJ

1 Place the sweet potatoes in a saucepan of water, bring to a boil, and cook for about 15 minutes until soft. Drain the potatoes and return them to the saucepan.

2 Mash the potatoes with all the other ingredients and serve immediately.

FRUITY COUSCOUS
with lime

Preparation time: 5 minutes

Cooking time: 12 minutes

Serves 4

1⅔ cups Vegetable Stock (see page 14)

1⅛ cup couscous

1 tablespoon olive oil

1 red onion, chopped

1 red bell pepper, cored, seeded, and chopped

3 tablespoons chopped flat-leaf parsley

3 tablespoons torn basil leaves

3 tablespoons chopped mint

juice and zest of 1 lime

3 tablespoons chopped dried apricots

pinch of ground cinnamon

¼ cup toasted slivered almonds

CARBOHYDRATE 36 g

FAT 7 g

PROTEIN 6 g

ENERGY 223 kcal/930 kJ

1 Heat the vegetable stock in a pan with a lid. Add the couscous, cover, and leave to swell for about 6 minutes.

2 Meanwhile, heat the oil in a skillet and gently soften the onion and bell pepper over a moderate heat for 3 minutes.

3 Stir the cooked onion and bell pepper into the couscous with all the other ingredients. Heat through for 5 minutes and serve hot or cold.

Nutrition note

Couscous makes a refreshing change to rice and it offers a medium GI rating.

CUCUMBER AND TOMATO SALSA

Preparation time: 10 minutes

Serves 4

6-inch piece of cucumber, finely diced

1 orange bell pepper, cored, seeded, and finely chopped

2 scallions, green stems only, finely sliced

6 vine-ripened tomatoes, finely diced

juice of 1 lime

2 tablespoons chopped flat-leaf parsley

2 tablespoons chopped mint

salt and black pepper

CARBOHYDRATE 7 g

FAT 1 g

PROTEIN 2 g

ENERGY 36 kcal/155 kJ

1 Mix together the cucumber, orange bell pepper, scallions, and tomatoes.

2 Make a dressing by combining the lime juice, herbs, and seasoning.

3 Stir the dressing into the vegetables and pile into a serving bowl.

Nutrition note

The raw fruit and vegetables in this salsa are packed with vitamins, including vitamin C and betacarotene, both of which are valuable antioxidants.

SAUTÉED OKRA
with onion seeds and saffron

Preparation time: 10 minutes

Cooking time: 25 minutes

Serves 4

3 tablespoons olive oil

1 teaspoon onion seeds

1 garlic clove, crushed

1 teaspoon crushed ginger

1 lb okra, topped and tailed

a good pinch of saffron

1 teaspoon curry powder

½ teaspoon salt

TO SERVE

2 teaspoons sesame seeds

2 tablespoons chopped cilantro leaves

CARBOHYDRATE 5 g

FAT 11 g

PROTEIN 4 g

ENERGY 129 kcal/536 kJ

1 Heat the oil in a nonstick pan and add the onion seeds. Fry over a moderate heat for a few seconds before stirring in the garlic and ginger.

2 Add the okra and flavorings and cook, uncovered, for about 20 minutes until tender. Stir occasionally. Add small amounts of hot water if the okra begin to stick to the bottom of the pan.

3 Serve immediately sprinkled with sesame seeds and cilantro leaves.

Nutrition note
Cooking for less time helps to keep the GI low because the okra are nearer their firm, raw state.

FIVE-MINUTE BABY SWEETCORN
with cilantro

Preparation time: 5 minutes

Cooking time: 5 minutes

Serves 4

1 teaspoon whole coriander seeds

1 tablespoon olive oil

8 oz baby sweetcorn

good pinch of black pepper

2 teaspoons ground turmeric

2 cups cilantro leaves, finely chopped

2 tablespoons lemon juice

CARBOHYDRATE 2 g

FAT 3 g

PROTEIN 2 g

ENERGY 48 kcal/198 kJ

1 Lightly crush the coriander seeds with a rolling pin or using a mortar and pestle. Heat the oil in a wok or skillet, add the coriander seeds, and stir-fry for a few seconds.

2 Stir in the sweetcorn with the black pepper and turmeric and cook for 3–4 minutes. Add the cilantro leaves.

3 Add the lemon juice and allow to sizzle in the pan just before serving.

Nutrition note

Baby sweetcorn, weight for weight, is lower in calories than sweetcorn kernels and maintains its crunchy texture in this recipe.

Delectable
Desserts

BAKED PEAR
with almond crisp

Preparation time: 10 minutes

Cooking time: 20 minutes

Serves 4

½ cup plus 2 tablespoons whole-wheat flour

⅔ cup ground almonds

½ cup light brown sugar

¼ cup butter

4 pears, unpeeled, quartered, cored, and sliced lengthwise

juice of 1 lime

2 tablespoons slivered almonds

¾ cup low-fat crème fraîche, to serve (optional)

CARBOHYDRATE 50 g

FAT 29 g

PROTEIN 8 g

ENERGY 483 kcal/2016 kJ

1 Mix the flour, ground almonds, and sugar together in a large bowl. Rub in the butter with your fingertips until it resembles fine breadcrumbs.

2 Arrange the pear slices in 4 tall, ovenproof ramekin dishes and drizzle with the lime juice.

3 Cover the pears with the crisp mixture and sprinkle over the slivered almonds.

4 Bake in a preheated 425°F oven for 20 minutes and serve warm, topped with the crème fraîche, if liked.

Nutrition notes

No additional sugar is added to the fruit in this recipe because the crisp topping provides more than enough sweetness.

Pears are a low-GI fruit. Cooking fruit until soft tends to raise its GI rating, so the pears in this recipe are cooked until only slightly softened. If you prefer them softer, cook them for a little longer.

Using ground almonds in the crisp mixture means you can reduce the quantity of butter you might traditionally use. In this way you replace some of the saturated fat from butter with healthier monounsaturated fats.

CHERRY GRANOLA
with macadamia nuts

Preparation time: 10 minutes

Serves 4

4 oz almond biscotti

2 tablespoons wheatgerm

¼ cup sunflower seeds

½ cup macadamia nuts, chopped

3 cups pitted Morello cherries in natural juice, drained

4 oz low-fat cream cheese

1 heaping cup low-fat plain, strained yogurt

½ oz bittersweet chocolate, (70% cocoa solids), roughly grated

CARBOHYDRATE 43 g

FAT 18 g

PROTEIN 12 g

ENERGY 380 kcal/1586 kJ

1 Place the almond biscotti in a plastic bag and use a rolling pin to crush them roughly.

2 Add the wheatgerm, sunflower seeds, and macadamia nuts to the crushed biscotti and mix.

3 Divide the biscotti mixture evenly among 4 dessert glasses or small serving dishes. Top each biscotti base with the drained cherries.

4 In a bowl, beat together the cream cheese and yogurt until well combined. Spoon the mixture over the cherries. Sprinkle over the grated chocolate before serving.

Nutrition note

Fresh cherries have a GI of 22. This, combined with the nuts, seeds, wheatgerm (a great source of vitamin E and folic acid), a low-fat creamy layer, and an antioxidant-rich dark chocolate topping, makes a healthy but luscious dessert.

OATMEAL AND RASPBERRIES

Preparation time: 10 minutes

Cooking time: 5 minutes

Serves 4

1½ cups rough pinhead oatmeal

1 scant cup low-fat plain, strained yogurt

2½ oz mascarpone cheese

2 tablespoons whiskey

1⅔ cups raspberries

CARBOHYDRATE 66 g

FAT 10 g

PROTEIN 8 g

ENERGY 257 kcal/1080 kJ

1 Toast the pinhead oatmeal in a dry nonstick skillet over medium-low heat for 4–5 minutes until it is slightly brown. Shake regularly to prevent burning.

2 Mix the yogurt together with the mascarpone and whiskey.

3 Assemble the dessert in layers in 4 dessert glasses. Start with a base of oatmeal, followed by raspberries, and then the whiskey-flavored yogurt. Reserve 4 raspberries and some toasted oatmeal to sprinkle on top as a garnish.

Nutrition notes

Oatmeal has been shown to help regulate blood levels of fats and sugars because it is high in soluble fiber and low in GI.

The raspberries in this dish provide a good source of vitamin C, an antioxidant vitamin.

BITTER CHOCOLATE ALMOND MOUSSE

Preparation time: 20 minutes, plus chilling

Cooking time: 5 minutes

Serves 6

5 oz bittersweet chocolate, minimum 70% cocoa solids, broken into small pieces

5 oz silken tofu, drained

⅓ cup ground almonds

1 tablespoon almond liqueur

scant ¼ cup confectioners' sugar

whites of 3 large eggs

1 tablespoon toasted slivered almonds, to garnish

CARBOHYDRATE 21 g

FAT 12 g

PROTEIN 6 g

ENERGY 214 kcal/894 kJ

1 Melt the chocolate slowly in a bowl set over a pan of hot (not boiling) water. Do not let the bowl touch the water and do not let steam form because this will affect the smoothness of the chocolate.

2 Put the melted chocolate, tofu, ground almonds, almond liqueur, and confectioners' sugar in a blender and mix together.

3 Whisk the egg whites until they hold soft peaks. Add one-third of the chocolate mixture and stir to distribute it evenly.

4 Lightly fold the rest of the chocolate mixture into the whisked egg whites and divide the mixture among 4 dessert or wine glasses. Cover with plastic wrap and chill for 2–3 hours.

5 Sprinkle over toasted almonds before serving.

Nutrition notes

Tofu is made from soy beans and contains isoflavones, which are associated with the improvement of bone health and the prevention of heart disease. It is also particularly beneficial in reducing the symptoms of hot flashes in menopausal women.

Chocolate with a high cocoa content is rich in flavonoids and antioxidants, which are also good for your heart.

CHINESE SPICED CITRUS SALAD

Preparation time: 15 minutes, plus chilling

Cooking time: 15 minutes

Serves 4

3 oranges, peeled and pith removed, separated into segments

1 ruby grapefruit, peeled and pith removed, separated into segments

1 banana, thinly sliced

¾ cup low-fat crème fraîche, to serve

SYRUP

1 whole clove

¼ teaspoon five spice powder

zest of 1 lime

1 vanilla pod, split lengthwise

¼ teaspoon grated ginger root

1¼ cups water

TO GARNISH

1 tablespoon finely chopped mint

seeds of 1 pomegranate

CARBOHYDRATE 25 g

FAT 6 g

PROTEIN 4 g

ENERGY 163 kcal/688 kJ

1 Prepare the syrup by combining all the ingredients in a nonstick pan. Bring to a boil and simmer gently for 3–5 minutes. Remove from the heat and leave to infuse and cool.

2 Meanwhile, mix the orange and grapefruit segments together in an attractive glass bowl. Add the banana.

3 Pour the cooled syrup through a sieve to remove the solids, then pour it over the fruits.

4 Leave the salad to chill in the refrigerator for 2–3 hours before serving with crème fraîche and garnishing with finely chopped mint and pomegranate seeds.

To remove pomegranate seeds Cut the pomegranate in half, insert a fork into one half, and twist. The seeds should fall out like jewels.

Nutrition note
Bursting with the antioxidant vitamin C, this citrus salad could be eaten as an appetizer, dessert, or even a sumptuous snack.

PRUNES IN MUSCAT
served with pistachio oaties

Preparation time: 15 minutes, plus marinating

Cooking time: 12–15 minutes

Serves 6

1⅓ cups ready-to-eat Agen prunes, pitted

6 tablespoons Muscat liqueur

⅔ cup low-fat plain, strained yogurt, to serve

PISTACHIO OATIES

scant ½ cup self-rising whole-wheat flour

½ cup rolled oats

½ cup unsalted pistachio nuts, crushed

2 tablespoons soft brown sugar

1 teaspoon ground cinnamon

zest from 1 orange

3 tablespoons butter

CARBOHYDRATE 36 g

FAT 11 g

PROTEIN 6 g

ENERGY 280 kcal/1184 kJ

1 Slit each prune in the center and arrange them in a shallow dish. Pour over the Muscat and leave to marinate.

2 Meanwhile, make the oaties. Mix together all the ingredients except the butter in a large bowl.

3 Melt the butter and add it to the dry ingredients. Combine these together and roll into 12 small balls. Add a little milk if the mixture is too dry.

4 Put the oaties on a nonstick cookie sheet and press down on each one to flatten. Bake in a preheated 400°F oven for 12–15 minutes until golden and then cool on a wire rack.

5 Serve the prunes with their marinade, topped with yogurt and accompanied by the pistachio oaties.

Nutrition notes

These small, granola-style cookies are packed with fiber, which helps promote healthy digestion.

Prunes are high in iron and have a GI of only 29.

RICOTTA AND CHOCOLATE TRIFLE

Preparation time: 15 minutes, plus chilling

Serves 4

3½ oz almond biscotti

⅓ cup orange juice

1 tablespoon brandy (optional)

heaping ¾ cup ricotta cheese

⅔ cup low-fat plain, strained yogurt

3 tablespoons confectioners' sugar

few drops of vanilla extract

1 oz bittersweet chocolate, minimum 70% cocoa solids, grated

⅔ cup blueberries

CARBOHYDRATE 42 g

FAT 11 g

PROTEIN 9 g

ENERGY 297 kcal/1247 kJ

1 Soak the biscotti in the orange juice and brandy, if using.

2 Meanwhile, beat the ricotta together with the yogurt, confectioners' sugar, and vanilla extract until smooth and creamy.

3 Spoon the soaked biscotti into the base of 4 glass sundae dishes. Divide half the cheese mixture among the glasses. Top with half the grated chocolate and then the blueberries. Spoon the remaining cheese mixture into the dishes and finish with a semicircle of grated chocolate. Chill for at least 30 minutes before serving.

Nutrition notes

Chocolate does well on the GI front, and it is always best to choose a chocolate with a high percentage of cocoa solids.

Adding low-fat plain, strained yogurt to the ricotta cheese helps keep down the fat content.

PINEAPPLE CREOLE WEDGES

Preparation time: 10 minutes

Cooking time: 10 minutes

Serves 4

1 small pineapple, about 2½ lb
1 tablespoon dark rum
juice of 1 lime
1 tablespoon sesame seeds

CARBOHYDRATE 32 g
FAT 3 g
PROTEIN 2 g
ENERGY 159 kcal/679 kJ

1 Cut the pineapple lengthwise, first in half and then into quarters, leaving the leaves intact. The wedges should be about ½ inch thick, so it may be necessary to divide them again.

2 Mix together the dark rum and lime juice and sprinkle the mixture over the pineapple slices.

3 Toast the pineapple under a preheated hot broiler for 8–10 minutes, turning to ensure even cooking.

4 Serve sprinkled with sesame seeds.

Nutrition note
Sesame seeds are rich in protein, iron, and zinc and help bring down the GI rating of this dessert.

LAYERED STRAWBERRIES
with mint, crème fraîche, and pecans

Preparation time: 15 minutes

Cooking time: 1 minute

Serves 4

⅓ cup pecans, roughly chopped, reserving 4 halves

2¼ cups low-fat crème fraîche

1 tablespoon honey

1 kiwifruit, peeled and sliced

1 cup plus 2 tablespoons strawberries, sliced, reserving 4 unsliced with leaves

2 tablespoons shredded mint, plus 4 small mint sprigs

CARBOHYDRATE 13 g

FAT 15 g

PROTEIN 4 g

ENERGY 196 kcal/813 kJ

1 Dry-roast the chopped pecans for 1 minute in a heavy pan and allow to cool.

2 Next, mix the crème fraîche with the honey and kiwifruit.

3 Layer the strawberries, shredded mint, chopped pecans, and crème fraîche in 4 dessert glasses. Repeat the layers and decorate the top with the reserved pecan halves, whole strawberries, and sprigs of mint. Serve chilled.

Nutrition note
Strawberries contain more vitamin C than any other berry.

BAKED SAFFRON PEACHES
with mango and cream

Preparation time: 15 minutes

Cooking time: 15 minutes

Serves 4

2 large, slightly underripe peaches, halved and pitted

2 tablespoons pistachio nuts, halved

a few saffron threads

a few drops almond extract

¼ cup crunchy oat cereal

2 tablespoons orange juice

2-inch cinnamon stick, broken into 8 pieces

TO SERVE

⅓ cup light cream

½ slightly underripe mango, thinly sliced

1 teaspoon bittersweet chocolate, minimum 70% cocoa solids, grated (optional)

CARBOHYDRATE 16 g

FAT 6 g

PROTEIN 3 g

ENERGY 130 kcal/547 kJ

1 Scoop some of the peach out of the peach halves and chop this finely. Put the halved peaches, skin-side down, in a lightly oiled baking dish.

2 Mix together the chopped peach flesh, pistachios, saffron, almond extract, oat cereal, and orange juice. Spoon this mixture carefully into the peach halves.

3 Push the cinnamon stick pieces into the peach halves. Bake the peaches uncovered in a preheated 350°F oven for 15 minutes.

4 Carefully arrange one peach half on each dessert plate and pour some of the cream over one side of the peach. Serve with mango slices and a sprinkling of chocolate, if using.

Nutrition note

Choosing slightly underripe fruit helps to keep the GI low. The peaches would normally be baked in the oven for 20–25 minutes, but the softer the cooked fruit, the higher the GI, so this recipe bakes the fruit until they are just cooked.

SIZZLING BANANAS
with orange zest and pistachio nuts

Preparation time: 5 minutes

Cooking time: 5 minutes

Serves 4

2 tablespoons butter

4 bananas, halved lengthwise

zest and juice of 1 large orange

2 tablespoons chopped pistachio nuts

3 tablespoons low-fat plain, strained yogurt,
to serve

CARBOHYDRATE 28 g

FAT 11 g

PROTEIN 5 g

ENERGY 230 kcal/960 kJ

1 Melt the butter gently in a large, nonstick skillet, being careful not to let it brown. Add the bananas, cut-side down, and cook for 1–2 minutes, using 2 wooden spoons to turn them over.

2 Add the orange zest and pistachio nuts, increasing the heat a little, so that the bananas turn brown and crisp on the outside.

3 Just before serving, drizzle over the orange juice and serve, still sizzling, with the yogurt.

Nutrition note
Both the nuts and the orange help to lower the glycemic index of this dessert.

PLUM AND PEACH BRUSCHETTA

Preparation time: 15 minutes, plus marinating

Cooking time: 25 minutes

Serves 4

4 peaches, skinned, halved, and pitted

4 large red plums, halved and pitted

¼ cup brandy

1 tablespoon unsalted butter

4 slices sourdough bread, each about ¾ inch thick

TO SERVE

1 vanilla pod, seeds scraped out

¾ cup low-fat crème fraîche

CARBOHYDRATE 39 g

FAT 10 g

PROTEIN 6 g

ENERGY 287 kcal/1208 kJ

1 Put the peach and plum halves in a bowl with the brandy and marinate for 20 minutes.

2 Mix the vanilla seeds into the crème fraîche. Leave to infuse.

3 Butter each slice of bread on one side and lay in a large ovenproof dish. On each piece of bread press 2 halves of peach, cut-side down. Add plums, cut-side up, to the bread and pour on any juices from the bowl.

4 Bake in a preheated 400°F oven for 25 minutes. The bread should be crisp on the edges and the fruit cooked. Serve with the vanilla crème fraîche.

Nutrition note

Fruit is high in the antioxidant vitamins A and C, which are beneficial for heart health and may help prevent cancer.

HOT BERRIES
with orange cream

Preparation time: 15 minutes

Cooking time: 8 minutes

Serves 4

⅔ cup low-fat plain, strained yogurt

½ cup light cream

1 egg yolk

1 teaspoon orange-blossom water

1 orange, peeled and pith removed, separated into segments

1 heaping cup blueberries

1 cup strawberries, cut into bite-sized pieces

CARBOHYDRATE 13 g

FAT 9 g

PROTEIN 5 g

ENERGY 143 kcal/595 kJ

1 Mix together the yogurt, cream, egg yolk, and orange-blossom water.

2 Mix the orange segments with the blueberries and strawberries.

3 Put a mixture of each fruit in ovenproof serving dishes and spoon the sauce over to cover the fruit.

4 Place under a preheated hot broiler for 5–8 minutes, until the cream starts to bubble and turn brown.

5 Serve immediately, being sure to warn your guests about the hot dishes.

Nutrition note

Fresh fruit is an excellent source of vitamin C and fiber. Creating a recipe from fruit helps add interest if you're someone who doesn't like munching your way through an apple.

INDEX

Author's Acknowledgment

A big thank you goes to my friend and colleague, Elaine Gardner, for her creativity and originality in helping me with these recipes.

To find out more about the author and her work visit her website **www.azminagovindji.com**

Publisher's Acknowledgments

Executive Editor Nicola Hill

Project Editor Leanne Bryan

Executive Art Editor Jo MacGregor

Design Ginny Zeal

Photographer Lis Parsons

Senior Production Controller Manjit Sihra

Picture Researcher Jennifer Veall